Primary Partners®
Sharing Time

I'll Follow Him in Faith

12 Learning Activities and Bite-size Memorize Scripture Posters
Preview of *Sharing Time Treasures*, 55 More Learning Activities to Match Theme
Preview of Other Activities, Songs, and Videos to Match Theme

"I'll Follow Him in Faith"   Sharing Time Themes 1-12
(see Table of Contents)

Introducing the Author and Illustrator, Creators of the Following Series of Books and CD-ROMS:

PRIMARY PARTNERS®:

Curriculum-based Manuals: *Nursery Vol. 1 & 2, CTR-A, CTR-B, Book of Mormon, Doctrine & Covenants, New Testament, Old Testament, Faith-in-God We Love Activity Days,* and *Super Fun Activity Days*

Current Sharing Time Theme: *Sharing Time, Sharing Time Treasures, Singing Fun*
Also, *Primary Songs Sing-Along* video by Bowden, illustrated by Jennette Guymon-King

FAMILY HOME EVENING:

File-Folder Family Home Evenings and *Homespun Fun Family Home Evenings* Vol. 1 & 2

YOUNG WOMEN:

Young Women Fun-tastic—Activities for Church manuals 1-3 and
Young Women Fun-tastic—Personal Progress Motivators

COLORED & READY-TO-USE GAMES & ACTIVITIES FOR FHE & PRIMARY:

Gospel Activities Series: Gospel Fun Activities, Fun in a Flash, Tons of Fun, and *Jesus Loves Me*
Singing-Motivators Series: Super Little Singers and *Super Singing Activities*
Gospel Games Series: Gospel Games and *Funner Than Fun*
(*2007 release)

Mary Ross, Author

Jennette Guymon-King, Illustrator

Mary Ross is an energetic mother and has been a Primary teacher and Relief Society president. She loves to help children and young women have a good time while learning. She has studied acting, modeling, and voice. Her varied interests include writing, creating activities and children's parties, and cooking. Mary and her husband Paul live with their daughter Jennifer in Sandy, Utah.

Jennette Guymon-King studied graphic arts and illustration at Utah Valley State College and the University of Utah. She served a mission in Japan. She enjoys sports, reading, cooking, art, gardening, and freelance illustrating. Jennette and her husband Clayton live in Bluffdale, Utah. They are the proud parents of their daughters Kayla Mae and Shelby, and sons Levi and Carson.

*Primary Partners® Sharing Time:
I'll Follow Him in Faith*
ISBN 978-1-59811-202-3

ACKNOWLEDGMENTS: Thanks to Inspire Graphics (www.inspiregraphics.com) for the use of Lettering Delights computer fonts for some activities.

Table of Contents

Primary Partners® Sharing Time
"I'll Follow Him in Faith"

INTRODUCTION
Primary Partners
SHARING TIME
Theme: I'll Follow Him in Faith

This volume of teaching ideas can be used year after year for Primary Sharing Time as well as for family home evening to teach children to follow Jesus Christ in faith.

The lessons will increase a child's faith in Jesus as they learn who He is, follow His example, and keep His commandments. They will learn that He is their Savior and Redeemer and that His gospel was restored in these the latter-days. They will be encouraged to keep their baptismal covenants, listen to the Holy Ghost, serve others, and share the gospel. They will learn to express thanks for their blessings and prepare for when Jesus comes again.

Bite-size Memorize

Follow me, and do the things which ye have 👁 👁 +n me do.

2 Nephi 31:12

If you use these for family home evening, they will help reinforce what children are learning in Primary—so let children teach you.

Simply copy, color, laminate, and cut out the activity visuals, then follow the instructions. Or print the patterns and instructions shown in this book in color or black-and-white from the CD-ROM (shown below).

Teaching couldn't be easier with these 12 post-and-present activities and Bite-size Memorize posters (see left) that represent the 12 "I'll Follow Him in Faith" themes. Reduce the Bite-size Memorize posters to hand out, or print them from the CD-ROM (in the full or reduced size).

Other teaching books and CD-ROMs created for the 2007 Sharing Time theme ("I'll Follow Him in Faith") are detailed in the back of this book. They are *Primary Partners Sharing Time Treasures* (55 activities for the twelve themes for 2007), *Primary Partners Singing Fun!*, and *Primary Sing-Along* video or DVD featuring songs for the 2007 year. You'll also find full-color books and CD-ROMs with ready-to-tear-out-and-use activities in *Jesus Loves Me—Gospel Fun Activities*, *Gospel Fun Activities*, *Tons of Fun—Gospel Activities*, and *Fun in a Flash—Gospel Activities*. Singing leaders, don't miss the other full-color ready-to-use books and CD-ROMs: *Super Singing Activities* and *Super Little Singers*.

Theme 1   I Have Faith in the Lord Jesus Christ

Scripture to Memorize:

Memorize *Alma 32:21* using visual shown right.

Song:

Sing "I'll Follow Him in Faith" in the *Friend,* Jan. 2003, 24, or p. 11 in the *Sacrament Meeting Presentation* outline. The song is illustrated in the *Primary Partners® Singing Fun!—I'll Follow Him in Faith* book and CD-ROM and in the *Sing-Along* video.

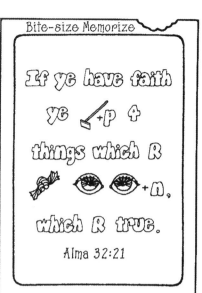

Activity: Smooth Sailing Game

OBJECTIVE—To Strengthen Faith: Help children learn actions that will help them stay afloat or sail smoothly as Nephi did when he showed faith and courage. Nephi helped save his family from the storms at sea by praying and by keeping Heavenly Father's commandments. Read *More Lesson Ideas* #3-4 on the following page.

TO MAKE VISUALS:

1. Copy, color, and cut out ship parts A and B, water-scene parts A and B, and fish that follow. Put the parts together as instructed on the graphics.

2. Mount water scene vertically on the bottom of a blue, half-size poster (as shown) and laminate the entire poster. Also laminate ship and fish.

3. The ship will move between the poster and a plastic protector sheet (as for photos). Cover water scene with plastic by cutting the clear plastic protector sheet (8 ½" x 11") along the bottom and left side to open and lay flat. Place the sheet over the front of the sea scene and secure sides (with tape or glue) to the back edges of the poster, leaving the top and bottom of the plastic protector open to insert ship between water scene and plastic.

4. Place double-stick or folded tape on the back of the top sail, placing the ship between water scene and plastic protector (place the ship bottom on the START position in the center of the poster). During the game, you will move the ship up or down on the poster (use new tape as needed).

5. Place fish in a container to draw from or create a fishing pole where leaders can paperclip fish to the line. To make the pole, tie a 30-inch string to a wooden dowel, pole, or stick and tie a paper clip to the bottom of string. Then, when children go to fish, the leader can paper-clip fish to string. Children can toss the fishing line over a sheet or blanket that has been draped over a rope line.

ACTIVITY:

1. Place bottom of ship in the center of the poster (using double-stick tape). Move the ship up and down (moving tape) as you talk about the objective on page 1, and tell the story found in 1 Nephi 18:9-15, 21. See also *More Lesson Ideas* #4 (below). Say, "We can increase our faith like Nephi and sail safely to our heavenly home as Nephi and his family sailed safely to the promised land. Our faith will grow stronger as we pray and keep God's commandments." See *More Lesson Ideas* #1.

2. Tell children, "In the story of Nephi and his family crossing the sea to the promised land, we learn that as long as they were keeping the commandments, the Liahona (compass) worked and they were guided while on the sea. When Nephi's brothers did not do these things, the Liahona stopped working and they were in danger of being drowned at sea. Because Nephi was faithful, his prayers were answered; the bands Laman and Lemuel placed on his hands and ankles were loosened, and Nephi could take care of his family. His faith had saved them."

3. Move the ship up and down to indicate a smooth or rough sail as follows, telling children, "Like Nephi's brothers, who did not keep the commandments and were in danger of sinking spiritually (and sinking the ship as well), we are in danger of sinking spiritually if we do not pray and keep the commandments. If we do keep the commandments, we can sail smoothly."

4. Place the ship in the center of the poster on the START position. Have children take turns drawing a fish card from a container or fishing for it with a pole and handing it to a leader to read aloud.

5. Once the leader has read the action, without the leader reading the consequences, e.g., STAY AFLOAT or SINK, have children guess what the consequences would be. Then leader reads the consequence. Have child move the ship up or down according to the consequence, then mount the fish on the outside of the plastic sheet protector with double-stick or folded tape.

6. If child draws a CHANCE fish, before reading the action, the leader asks the child to take a chance and guess if the action on the card will help them "stay afloat," or "sink." Then the leader reads the action. If the child guessed correctly, they move the ship up one, or if they guessed incorrectly, they move the ship down, regardless of the action on the card.

Reaching the Top or Bottom: If the ship reaches the highest or lowest level, stop and talk about where you are: (1) highest level, congratulate children for praying and keeping the commandments and sailing smoothly, (2) lowest level, tell them they have drowned in the depths of the sea for not praying and keeping the commandments. Then move the ship back onto the START position and continue until all cards are read.

More Lesson Ideas (teach the theme using the concepts below and the above activity):

1. **I have faith in the Lord Jesus Christ. Faith means trust. I trust Him, and I will follow Him** (Alma 32; Ether 12:12-18; "Faith," *True to the Faith*, 54-56; *Gospel Principles*, chapter 18). Read Alma 32:21, 28-30, to teach the principle of faith (trust in the Lord Jesus Christ). Teach children how to help their faith grow (John 5:39; John 7:16-17; James 1:5; Moroni 10:4-5; and D&C 21:4-5). Testify of how your faith has grown (Alma 32:27). Sing "Faith" in *Children's Songbook*, 96-97.

2. **My faith in Jesus Christ is the first principle of the gospel** (Articles of Faith 1:4; Matthew 8:5-13; Mark 10:46-52; Jeffrey R. Holland, "Abide in Me," *Ensign*, May 2004, 30-32).

3. **My faith in Jesus Christ is strengthened when I pray** (1 Nephi 7:16-18; 18:8-23; Enos 1:12-15; Mosiah 24:7-25; Alma 33:1-14; "Prayer," *True to the Faith*, 118-23).

4. **I have faith in the Lord Jesus Christ. He will help me keep the commandments** (1 Nephi 3:7). Dramatize the story of Nephi and his family building the ship—sailing to the promised land (1 Nephi 17-18). See also *Teaching, No Greater Call*, 165-66. Read 1 Nephi 3:7 and sing "Nephi's Courage" in *Children's Songbook*, 120-121. More faith and obedience scriptures: 1 Samuel 17; Daniel 3; or 1 Nephi 3-4.

If ye have faith

ye +p 4

things which R

 +n,

which R true.

Alma 32:21

Cut carefully along the inside of the dotted line.

CHANCE:
The Spirit told
you that riding
your bike down
a certain hill was
not safe, but you
went anyway.
SINK

CHANCE:
You couldn't
wait to eat
the meal
mother made
and didn't bless
the food.
SINK

CHANCE:
You were in
trouble, so you
prayed for
comfort and
strength.
STAY AFLOAT

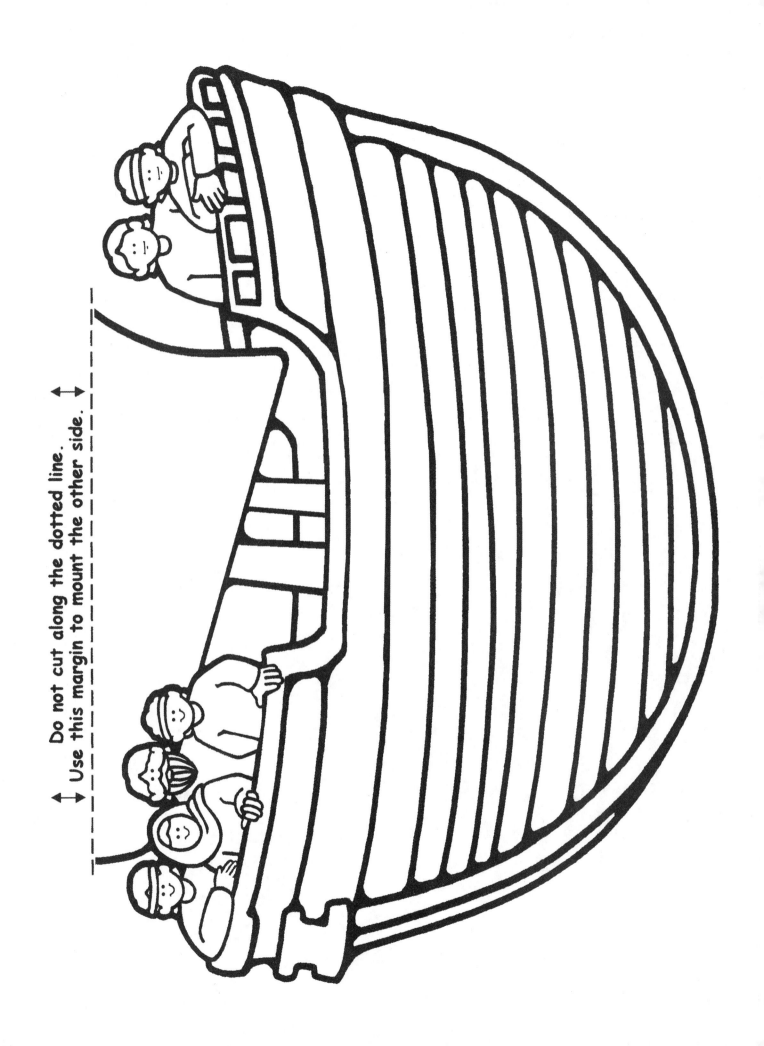

Do not cut along the dotted line.
Use this margin to mount the other side.

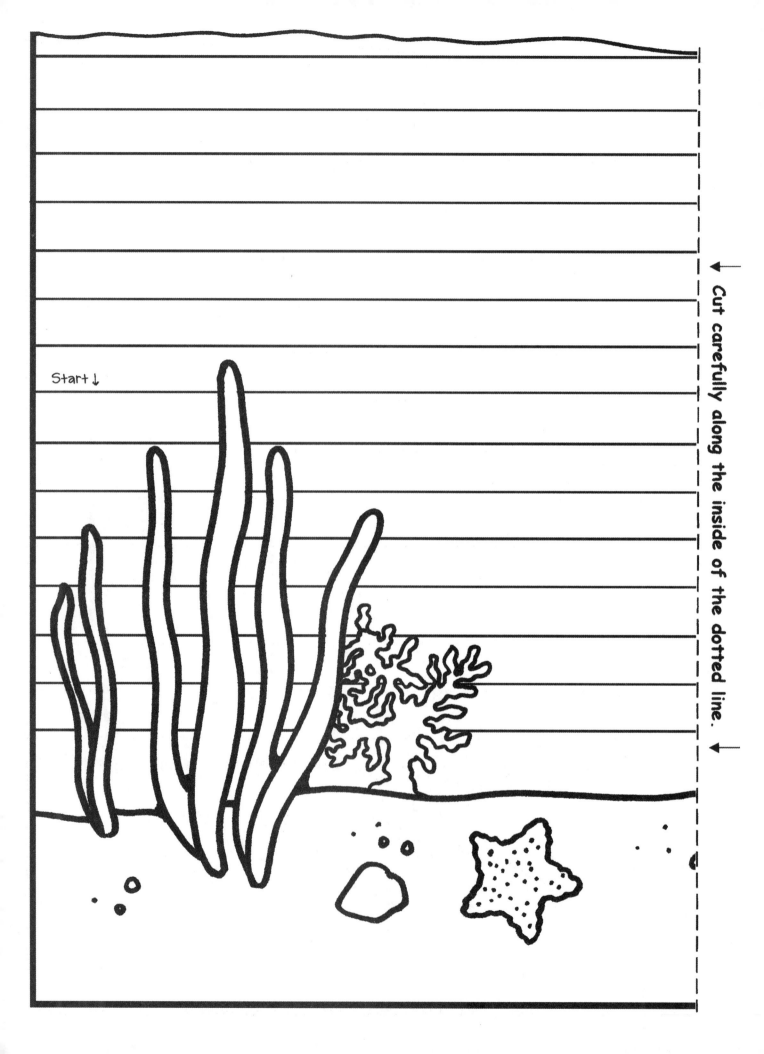

Start ↓

← Cut carefully along the inside of the dotted line. →

Kennedy's brother was in the way, and she didn't want him around when her friends came, but she was nice to him anyway and let him play. SAIL UP ONE.

Katie was turning eight and wanted to be baptized, even though her best friend was not a member and said not to. SAIL UP TWO.

Jessie felt bad about something he did. He didn't feel like praying or telling his parents what he did, but he did anyway. SAIL UP ONE.

Candice knew that loving others was a commandment, but she didn't really want to invite the new girl to her party. She invited her anyway. SAIL UP ONE.

Bridget wanted to buy a special toy at the store and would have enough money if she didn't pay her tithing, but she paid her tithing instead. SAIL UP TWO.

Eva's grandmother was not feeling good, so Eva knelt beside her bed and prayed for her. SAIL UP ONE.

Derrick knew that taking something that didn't belong to him was wrong, but he wanted a scooter. Derrick decided to save money to buy his own. SAIL UP ONE.

Brandon was baby-sitting the neighbor's children and saw some beer in the refrigerator. He wondered what it would taste like if he took a sip, but he closed the fridge instead. SAIL UP TWO.

Nicholas liked to thank others for things they had done, especially when he prayed to Heavenly Father. SAIL UP ONE.

Timmy's family wanted to read the scriptures just when his favorite TV show was on. He said, "Later," but later it was too late because it was time for bed. SINK DOWN ONE.

Missy knew that saying her morning prayers was important, but each morning she got up too late, rushed off to school, and didn't take the time to pray. SINK DOWN ONE.

Paisley's little sister was afraid of the dark and asked if she could sleep in Paisley's bed. Paisley thought prayer would help her sister feel better, but she sent her back to her room instead. SINK DOWN ONE.

Will's family called him for family prayer, but he didn't come on time, so he missed it. SINK DOWN TWO.

Megan's mother asked her to take care of the baby while she was away, but she decided to stay in her room and paint her nails instead. SINK DOWN TWO.

Shelby was excited to take her test at school because she could spell every word. The girl next to her asked her if she could see Shelby's answers, and Shelby said yes. SINK DOWN ONE.

Jayne's eyes wandered around the room when the family prayer was said, and she didn't hear her mother's beautiful prayer. SINK DOWN ONE.

Willy knew that if he skipped church on Sunday he would not learn about Jesus and how to choose the right, but he stayed home anyway. SINK DOWN ONE.

Stephanie's mother told her not to jump on the trampoline with more than one friend at a time, but it was her birthday, so she thought it didn't matter. SINK DOWN ONE.

Theme 2   My Faith in Jesus Christ Grows When I Know Who He is

Bite-size Memorize

And we 🐝🍃 and R sure t+🪐 thou art t+🪐 🧔 the ☀ of the living God.

John 6:69

Scripture to Memorize:

Memorize *John 6:69* using visual shown right.

Song:

Sing "This Is My Beloved Son" in the *Children's Songbook,* 76. The song is illustrated in the *Primary Partners® Singing Fun!—I'll Follow Him in Faith* book and CD-ROM and in the *Sing-Along* video.

Activity: Jesus' Life Puzzle

OBJECTIVE—To Know Jesus:
Children will learn how Jesus is the center of our life, and that He made our present life and our eternal life possible. Children's faith grows as they put together a puzzle that identifies eight things about Jesus. They will also learn of eight wonderful blessings they will receive because of Jesus. See *More Lesson Ideas #1-4* on the following page.

TO MAKE VISUALS: Copy, color, cut, and laminate 16 puzzle pieces and the Jesus center. You will need two posters to use as follows:
1. Mount the intact (uncut) puzzle on a poster, laminate the entire puzzle, and cut out the individual puzzle pieces.
2. Laminate an extra poster to assemble the puzzle on.

ACTIVITY:

1. Talk about Jesus, who is the Son of God, our Savior, Teacher, Brother, Creator, and Judge (shown on the center of puzzle). Review the puzzle pieces starting with the 11-o'clock "Jesus is Heavenly Father's Son" and moving clockwise. As you put the puzzle together one puzzle-set at a time, read the scriptures for each or talk about each (see below*).

2. Post the puzzle pieces randomly around the board. Have children take turns choosing pieces to make a match after placing Jesus in the center.

Scriptures:

1. Jesus is Heavenly Father's Son . . . so He is our brother (Mosiah 3:8).
2. Jesus created the earth for me . . . so I could learn to follow Him (Mosiah 4:2, starting with "we believe").
3. Jesus created me in His and Heavenly Father's image . . . so I can be like Them (D&C 20:18).
4. Jesus was baptized to show me the way . . . so I can return to heaven (Moses 6:52).
5. Jesus taught us the gospel . . . so we would know Heavenly Father's commandments (3 Nephi 18:10).
6. Jesus suffered for my sins . . . so I can repent and be forgiven (D&C 18:11).
7. Jesus was resurrected . . . so I can live again (Mosiah 15:20).
8. Jesus will be my judge . . . so I must make good choices (3 Nephi 27:16).

More Lesson Ideas (teach the theme using the concepts below and the above activity):

1. **Jesus Christ is Heavenly Father's firstborn Son. I am also a child of God** (D&C 93:21; Abraham 3:22-24; Acts 17:29; "I Lived in Heaven," *Children's Songbook*, 4; *Gospel Principles*, chapters 1-2).

2. **Heavenly Father has a plan for me. Jesus Christ and His Atonement are central to this plan** (Moses 6:62; "Atonement of Jesus Christ" and "Plan of Salvation," *True to the Faith*, 14-16, 115-17). Heavenly Father's plan is a journey that began in heaven. Teach about premortal life, earth life (physical bodies, families, gospel, ordinances, obedience, sin, and life after death). Teach about the spirit world, where our spirits wait for the resurrection. Sing "I Will Follow God's Plan," *Children's Songbook*, 164-65.

3. **Jesus created the earth as a place for us to live and gain experience** (3 Nephi 9:15; "Creation," *True to the Faith*, 44-45; *Gospel Principles*, chapter 5). Use "My Gospel Standards" to teach what we must do to return to live with Heavenly Father and Jesus Christ. Sing "I Want to Live the Gospel," *Children's Songbook*, 148.

4. **Jesus Christ lived on the earth. His teachings and miracles blessed the lives of the people** (Matthew 5-7, 9:18-35; 14:15-33; "Tell Me the Stories of Jesus," *Children's Songbook*, 57; Sydney S. Reynolds, "A God of Miracles," *Ensign*, May 2001, 12-13).

And we [bee]+[leaf] and R sure t+[hat] thou art t+[hat] [Christ] the [sun] of the living God.

John 6:69

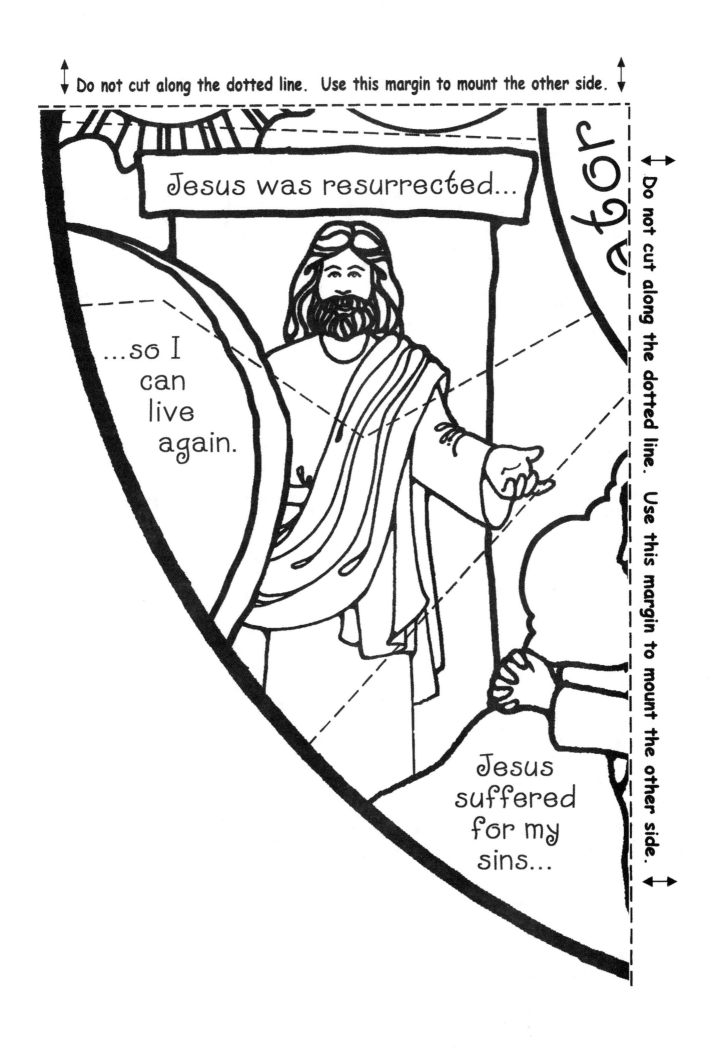

Theme 3 My Faith in Jesus Christ Grows When I Follow His Example and Keep His Commandments

Scripture to Memorize:

Memorize *2 Nephi 31:12* using visual shown right.

Song:

Sing "I'm Trying to Be like Jesus" in the *Children's Songbook*, 78-79. The song is illustrated in the *Primary Partners® Singing Fun!—I'll Follow Him in Faith* book and CD-ROM and in the *Sing-Along* video.

Activity: Sunny Sunday Activities

OBJECTIVE—To Honor the Sabbath: Help children understand which activities will help them keep the Gospel Standard "I will do the things on the Sabbath that will help me feel close to Heavenly Father and Jesus Christ" ("My Gospel Standards"). Read *More Lesson Ideas #3* on the following page.

TO MAKE VISUALS: Copy, color, and cut out the *Sunny Sunday* sun (yellow), *Gloomy Glum-day* circle (blue), Gospel Standard banner, sun rays and clouds, and wordstrips. Laminate them and cut them out. Laminate a mounting poster. Mount sun, circle, and sign on poster as shown. *Note:* Do not tape or glue sun sides to poster, to leave an opening where sun rays can be inserted (see #4 that follows).

ACTIVITY 1—*Forecasting the Weather:*

1. Tell children that Sunday can be a *Sunny Sunday* filled with activities that help you feel close to Heavenly Father and Jesus, or it can be a *Gloomy Glum-day* if you do activities that are not appropriate for the Sabbath. These activities are okay on other days, but Sunday is a special day. On Sunday, Heavenly Father wants us to rest from our labors, avoid making others work, spend time with our family, attend our church meetings, and do things that will help us keep the Gospel Standard (have children repeat) "I will do the things on the Sabbath that will help me feel close to Heavenly Father and Jesus Christ."

2. Place a sun ray on the sun and say, "Let's find activities that will brighten our sun, making the Sabbath a *Sunny Sunday.*" Place a cloud on the circle and say, "Lets identify activities that might make us sad for not keeping the Sabbath day, making it a *Gloomy Glum-day.*"

3. Tell children, counting on your fingers, "There are five questions we can ask to know if the activity will help us have a *Sunny Sunday.* Does it help me: (1) think of Jesus, (2) be reverent, (3) learn the gospel, (4) spend time with family, or (5) rest?"

4. Have children help you determine what their spiritual weather would be like on Sunday by the actions they choose. Have them come up one at a time, choose a wordstrip, and read it aloud. Then have them choose a sun ray, if the activity is a *Sunny Sunday* activity, and place the ray behind the sun (as shown). Or if it is a *Gloomy Glum-day* activity, have them place the cloud on or around the circle (as shown).

ACTIVITY 2—*Sunny Side-Up Voting:* Read wordstrip/activities again and have children vote on activities. Have all children vote or have individual classes come up and vote as follows:

Option 1—With a thumbs-up if it is a *Sunny Sunday* activity, and a thumbs-down if it is a *Gloomy Glum-day* activity.

Option 2—Say "warm" for *Sunny Sunday* or "cold" for *Gloomy Glum-day* activities.

Option 3—Smile for *Sunny Sunday* or frown for *Gloomy Glum-day* activities.

More Lesson Ideas (teach the theme using the concepts below and the above activity):

1. **Jesus Christ's life is an example to me** (John 13:15; 3 Nephi 18:24; "Following the Example of the Savior," *Family Home Evening Resource Book*, 105; "I'm Trying to Be like Jesus," *Children's Songbook*, 78-79; songs from "Jesus Christ—Example" in "Topics" index in *Children's Songbook*).

2. **I will study the scriptures and pray** (John 5:39; Matthew 14:23; Alma 37:37; "Search, Ponder, and Pray," *Children's Songbook*, 109; "Scripture Power," *Outline for Sharing Time*, 2006, 10-11; "Prayer," *True to the Faith*, 118-23).

3. **I will keep the Sabbath day holy** (Exodus 20:8; D&C 59:9-14; "Sabbath," *True to the Faith*, 145-47).

4. **I will keep the commandments and live now to be worthy to go to the temple** (*Primary 1*, lesson 26; "My Gospel Standards"; "Temples," *True to the Faith*, 170-74).

Cut carefully along the inside of the dotted line.

Sunny · Sun

Do not cut along the dotted line.   Use this margin to mount the other side.

I will do those things on the sabbath that will help me feel close to Heavenly Father and Jesus Christ.

-My Gospel Standards

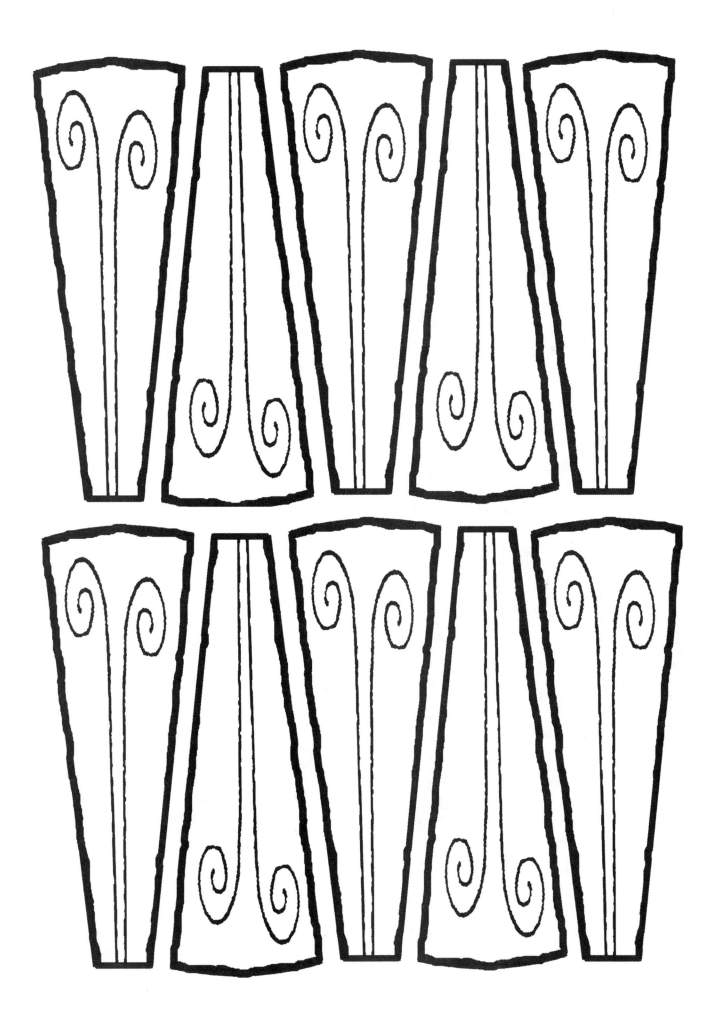

Cut carefully along the inside of the dotted line.

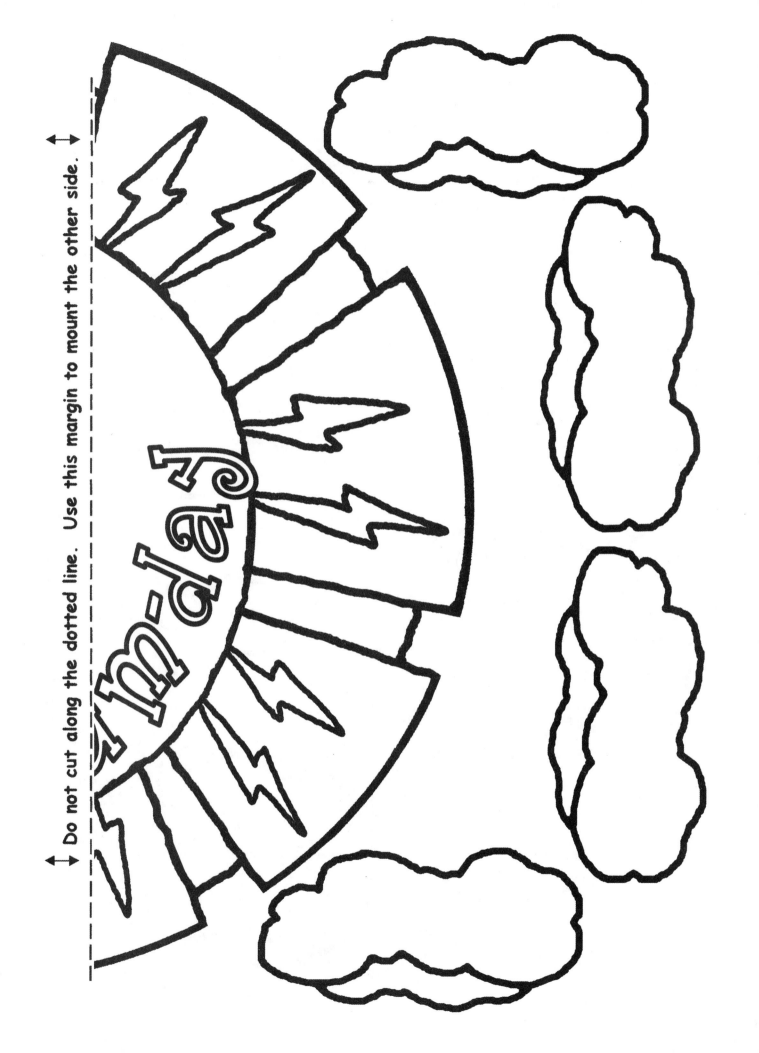

← Do not cut along the dotted line. Use this margin to mount the other side. →

Go for a short walk	Visit grandparents and the elderly	Go on a long hike	Do a kind deed
Take a nap	Go to the zoo	Read Church magazines	Pay your tithing
Help mow the lawn	Watch Church movies	Have a party with friends	Partake of sacrament reverently and remember Jesus
Write or draw pictures in your journal	Attend Primary reverently and learn about Jesus	Go to the movies	Sing hymns, Primary songs, or listen to Sunday music
Write letters or make cards to send to a missionary or family	Go out to eat	Make homemade treats with family	Help with dishes so you can talk and visit

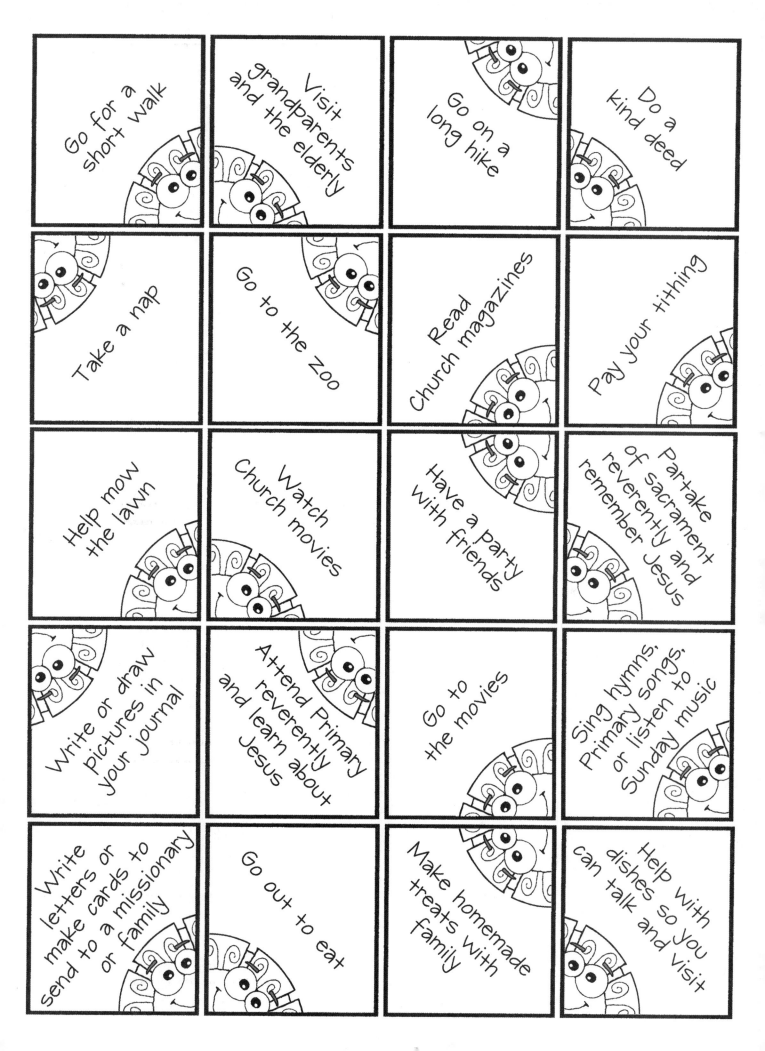

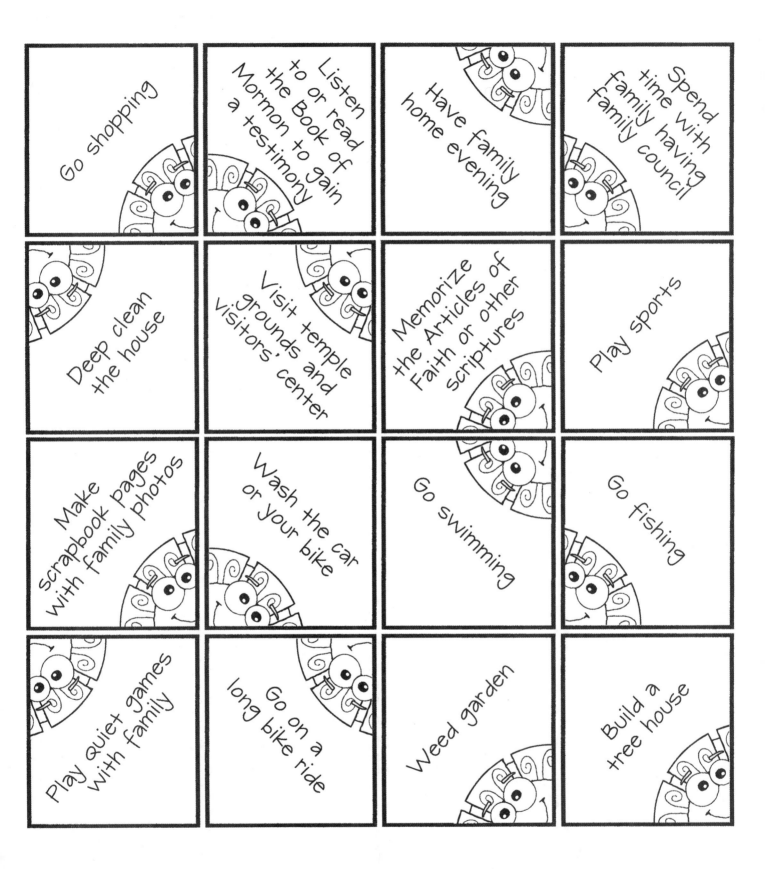

Go shopping

Listen to or read the Book of Mormon to gain a testimony

Have family home evening

Spend time with family having family council

Deep clean the house

Visit temple grounds and visitors' center

Memorize the Articles of Faith or other scriptures

Play sports

Make scrapbook pages with family photos

Wash the car or your bike

Go swimming

Go fishing

Play quiet games with family

Go on a long bike ride

Weed garden

Build a tree house

Theme 4   My Faith in Jesus Christ Grows
When I Know He Is My Savior and Redeemer

Bite-size Memorize

4 God so Love+ed the 🌐, t+🪐he gave his only 🐝+gotten ☀, t+🌿 🦉+soever 🐝+🌿eth in him should 🌾 🍐+ish, but have everlasting life. John 3:16

Scripture to Memorize:

Memorize *John 3:16* using visual shown right.

Song:

Sing "I Know That My Redeemer Lives" in *Hymns*, 136. The song is illustrated in the *Primary Partners® Singing Fun!—I'll Follow Him in Faith* book and CD-ROM and in the *Sing-Along* video.

Activity: Resurrection Miracles Match Game

OBJECTIVE—To Know That Jesus is Our Redeemer:
Children will learn about the miracle of the resurrection. They will learn that through His resurrection, Jesus made it possible for us to be resurrected and receive a perfect body. Read *More Lesson Ideas* #2 on the following page.

TO MAKE VISUALS: Copy, color, and cut out the images and match cards with two-part stories that follow. Laminate them and cut them out.

ACTIVITY:

1. Talk to children about the resurrection of Jesus, and tell them that because of Jesus, everyone who has died will be resurrected and receive a perfect body. Read and talk about:

> • Alma 40:23, "The soul shall be restored to the body, and the body to the soul; yea, and every limb and joint shall be restored to its body; yea, even a hair of the head shall not be lost; but all things shall be restored to their proper and perfect frame."
>
> • D&C 9:14, "Stand fast in the work wherewith I have called you, and a hair of your head shall not be lost, and you shall be lifted up at the last day."

2. Tell children that they are going to learn about those who have lived on the earth and passed on. They are now in the grave, but we have hope because of Jesus that they will live again. Read D&C 138:14, "All these had departed the mortal life, firm in the hope of a glorious resurrection, through the grace of God the Father and his Only Begotten Son, Jesus Christ."

3. Mount the match cards on the board with the first part of the card/story on the left and the second part of the card/story on the right. Have children take turns finding a card by matching up the body part and reading the story. Two children can team up and do this, each one reading their part of the card (with the child who retrieved the card on the left of the board reading his first).

4. Talk about each situation and how nice it will be when we can all be resurrected. If time, have children share stories of loved ones who have passed and why they will be happy when they are resurrected.

More Lesson Ideas (teach the theme using the concepts below and the above activity):

1. **Jesus Christ is my Savior and Redeemer. He came into the world to do the will of the Father** (2 Nephi 25:26; Luke 2:49 [41-49]; John 5:30 [17-30]; 3 Nephi 11:10-11; "Atonement of Jesus Christ," *True to the Faith,* 14-15; *Gospel Principles,* chapter 12; "He Sent His Son," *Children's Songbook,* 34-35).

2. **Because of the Atonement and Resurrection of Jesus Christ, I will be resurrected** (John 20:14-29; 1 Corinthians 15:20-22; Boyd K. Packer, "An Apostle Speaks to Children," *Friend,* July 1973, 32; "Universal Redemption from the Fall" and "Resurrection," *True to the Faith,* 18, 139-40).

3. **Because of the Atonement, I can repent and return to live with Heavenly Father and Jesus Christ** (1 John 2:25; D&C 19:16; "Repentance," *Children's Songbook,* 98; "Salvation from Our Sins," "The Gift of Eternal Life," and "Repentance," *True to the Faith,* 18-19, 132-35; *Gospel Principles,* chapter 19).

4. **My faith in Jesus Christ grows when I hear the apostles and prophets testify of Him** (D&C 1:38; 76:22-23; *Gospel Principles,* chapter 9).

4 God so (Love)ed the 🌍, t+🪐 he gave his only 🐝+gotten ☀, t+👒 🦉(Who)+soever 🐝+🍃+eth in him should 🍬 🍐+ish, but have everlasting life. John 3:16

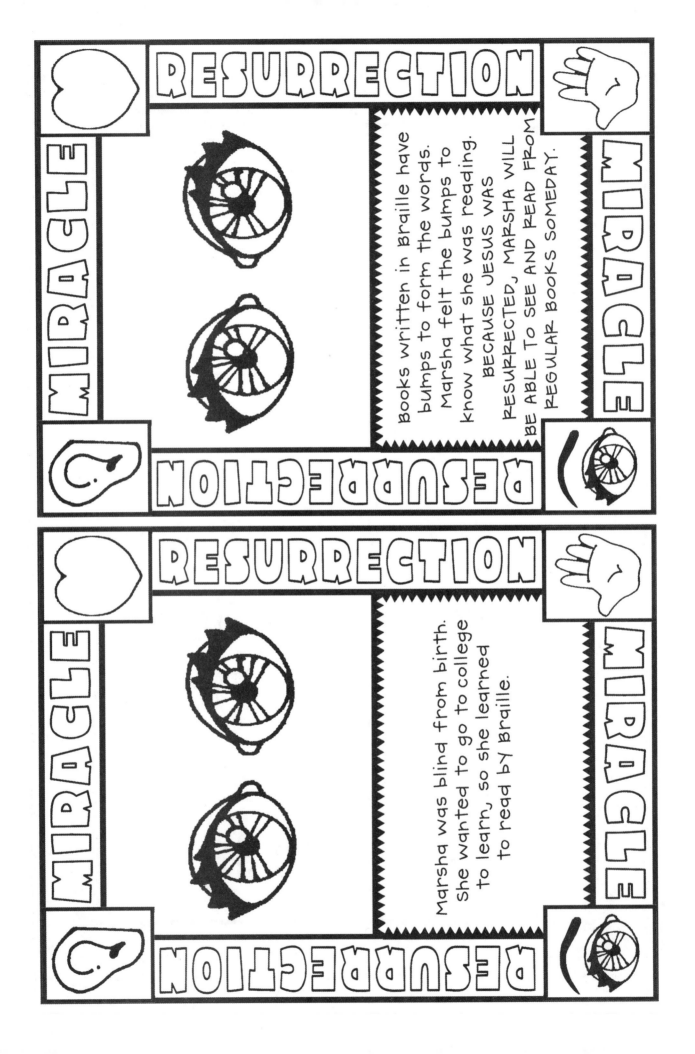

RESURRECTION

MIRACLE

MIRACLE

RESURRECTION

Books written in Braille have bumps to form the words. Marsha felt the bumps to know what she was reading. BECAUSE JESUS WAS RESURRECTED, MARSHA WILL BE ABLE TO SEE AND READ FROM REGULAR BOOKS SOMEDAY.

RESURRECTION

MIRACLE

MIRACLE

RESURRECTION

Marsha was blind from birth. She wanted to go to college to learn, so she learned to read by Braille.

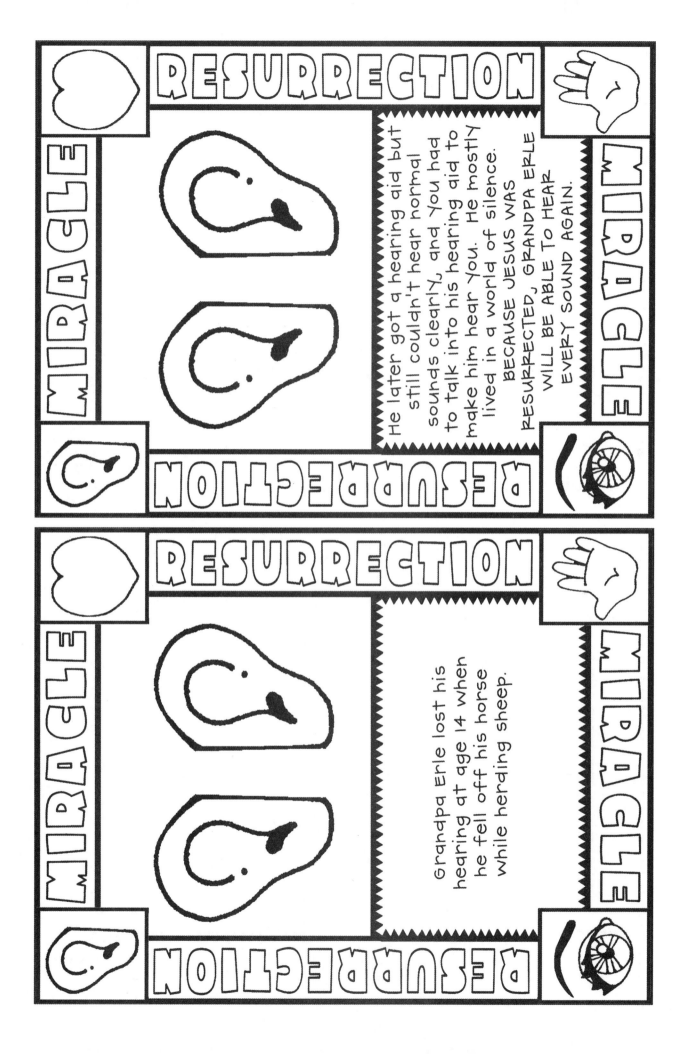

RESURRECTION

MIRACLE

He later got a hearing aid but still couldn't hear normal sounds clearly, and you had to talk into his hearing aid to make him hear you. He mostly lived in a world of silence.

BECAUSE JESUS WAS RESURRECTED, GRANDPA ERLE WILL BE ABLE TO HEAR EVERY SOUND AGAIN.

RESURRECTION

MIRACLE

Grandpa Erle lost his hearing at age 14 when he fell off his horse while herding sheep.

RESURRECTION

MIRACLE

MIRACLE

RESURRECTION

on the family farm he picked fruit with the one good hand. He also helped lift baskets of fruit onto the wagons going to market. BECAUSE JESUS WAS RESURRECTED, GLEN WILL RECEIVE THE HAND HE NEVER HAD.

RESURRECTION

MIRACLE

MIRACLE

RESURRECTION

Glen was always thankful for his body because he was born without his right hand. Even though Glen had difficulty doing things he always tried to do the best he could.

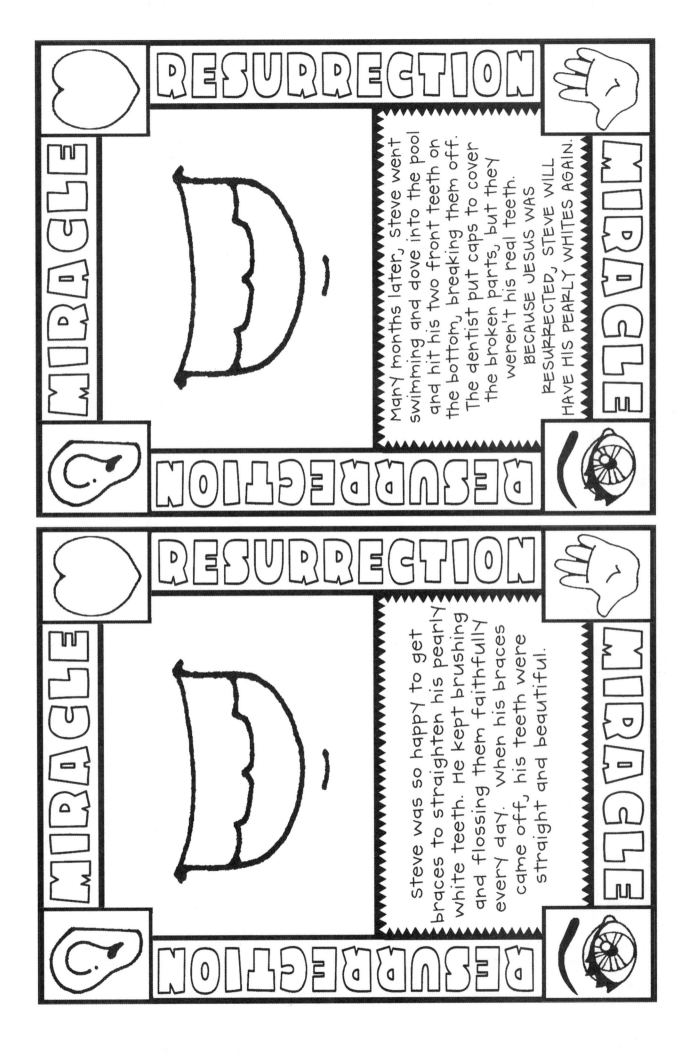

RESURRECTION

MIRACLE

MIRACLE

RESURRECTION

MIRACLE

Many months later, steve went swimming and dove into the pool and hit his two front teeth on the bottom, breaking them off. The dentist put caps to cover the broken parts, but they weren't his real teeth. BECAUSE JESUS WAS RESURRECTED, STEVE WILL HAVE HIS PEARLY WHITES AGAIN.

RESURRECTION

MIRACLE

MIRACLE

RESURRECTION

MIRACLE

Steve was so happy to get braces to straighten his pearly white teeth. He kept brushing and flossing them faithfully every day. When his braces came off, his teeth were straight and beautiful.

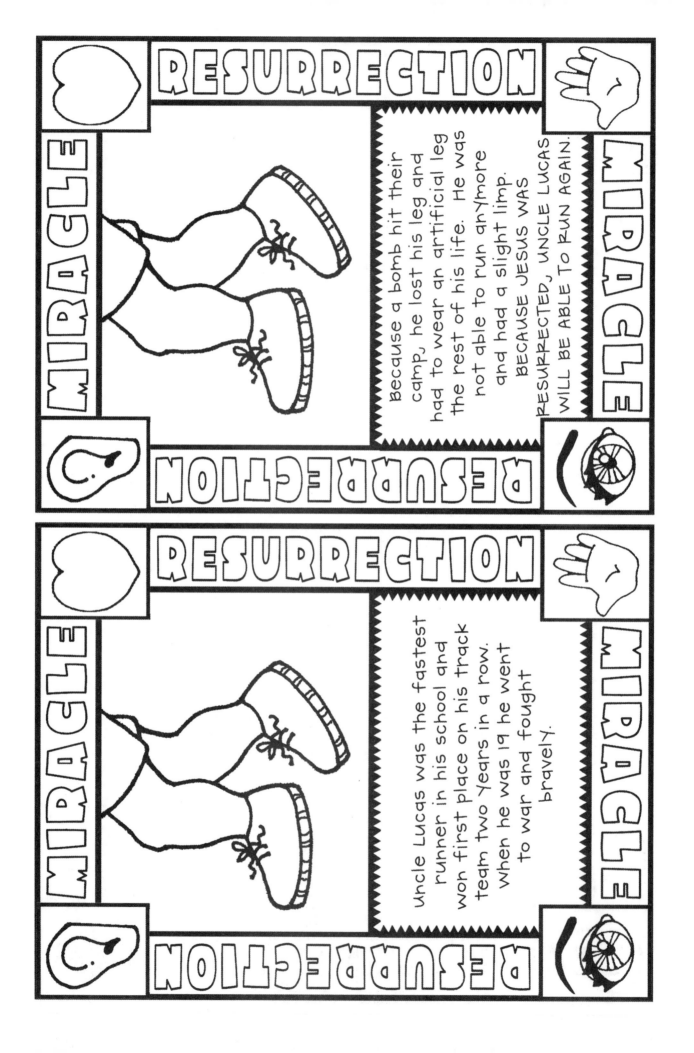

RESURRECTION

MIRACLE

MIRACLE

RESURRECTION

MIRACLE

Because a bomb hit their camp, he lost his leg and had to wear an artificial leg the rest of his life. He was not able to run anymore and had a slight limp. BECAUSE JESUS WAS RESURRECTED, UNCLE LUCAS WILL BE ABLE TO RUN AGAIN.

RESURRECTION

MIRACLE

MIRACLE

RESURRECTION

MIRACLE

Uncle Lucas was the fastest runner in his school and won first place on his track team two years in a row. When he was 19 he went to war and fought bravely.

RESURRECTION

MIRACLE

MIRACLE

RESURRECTION

One day grandpa got really sick with pneumonia. He lay in bed for a long time, got weaker and weaker, and finally died. BECAUSE JESUS WAS RESURRECTED, THE CHILDREN WILL BE ABLE TO BE WITH THEIR GRANDPA AGAIN.

RESURRECTION

MIRACLE

MIRACLE

RESURRECTION

Grandpa Hatch was the kids' favorite grandpa. He used to play checkers and other games with them. He would talk to them about their troubles and he knew just what to say.

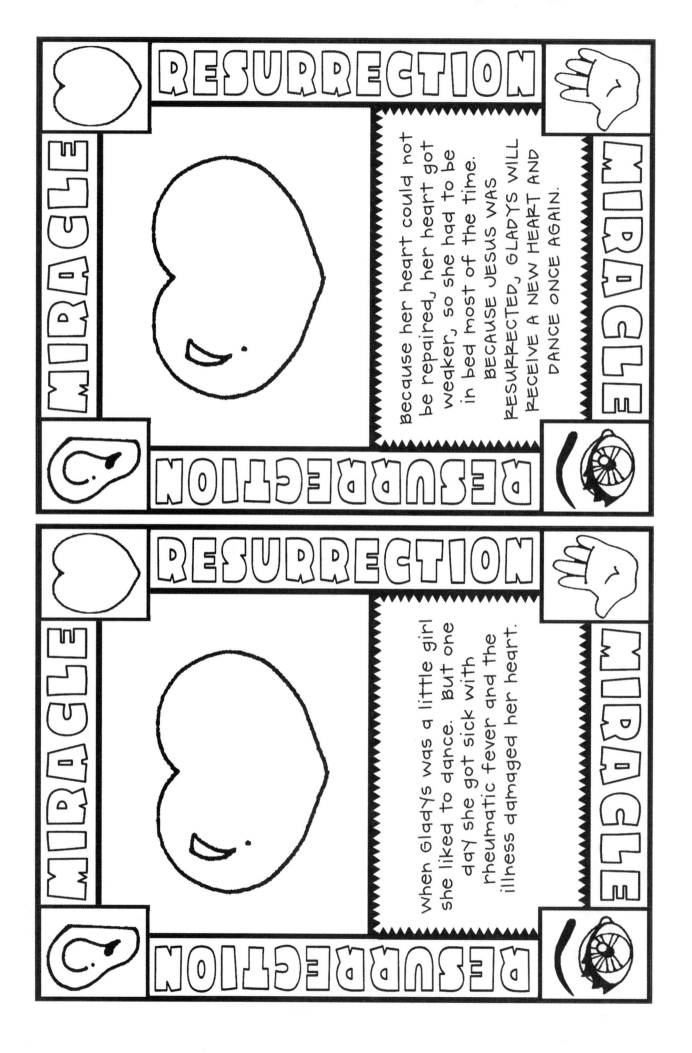

RESURRECTION

MIRACLE

MIRACLE

Because her heart could not be repaired, her heart got weaker, so she had to be in bed most of the time. BECAUSE JESUS WAS RESURRECTED, GLADYS WILL RECEIVE A NEW HEART AND DANCE ONCE AGAIN.

RESURRECTION

RESURRECTION

MIRACLE

MIRACLE

When Gladys was a little girl she liked to dance. But one day she got sick with rheumatic fever and the illness damaged her heart.

RESURRECTION

Card 1 (top):

RESURRECTION

MIRACLE

MIRACLE

RESURRECTION

The day the baby was born it died. The parents were very sad and prayed that they would be able to raise their baby girl someday.

BECAUSE JESUS WAS RESURRECTED, THE BABY WILL LIVE AGAIN AND HAVE A STRONG, PERFECT BODY.

Card 2 (bottom):

RESURRECTION

MIRACLE

MIRACLE

RESURRECTION

A mother gave birth to a baby too early and its lungs were not strong enough, so it couldn't breathe.

RESURRECTION

MIRACLE

MIRACLE

RESURRECTION

MIRACLE

For the rest of her life she couldn't smell the warm bread baking in the oven, the food she ate, or the beautiful roses she planted in her garden. BECAUSE JESUS WAS RESURRECTED, GREAT-GRANDMA STELLA WILL BE ABLE TO SMELL FOOD AND FLOWERS AGAIN.

RESURRECTION

MIRACLE

MIRACLE

MIRACLE

Great-grandma Stella was cleaning one day and mixed two cleaners together. When she sniffed the strong cleaners she lost her sense of smell.

RESURRECTION

RESURRECTION

RESURRECTION

MIRACLE

MIRACLE

RESURRECTION

One day otto got into a car accident and the car caught fire. otto's face was badly burned and scarred. He had plastic surgery to make it look better, but he wasn't the same.

Because Jesus was resurrected, otto will have his handsome face again.

RESURRECTION

MIRACLE

MIRACLE

RESURRECTION

otto was a good-looking young man, everyone said. People would stop and tell him he had a nice face.

Theme 5   My Faith in Jesus Christ Grows When I Learn about the Restoration of the Gospel

Scripture to Memorize:

Memorize *Isaiah 29:14* using visual shown right.

Song:

Sing "An Angel Came to Joseph Smith" in the *Children's Songbook*, 86. The song is illustrated in the *Primary Partners® Singing Fun!—I'll Follow Him in Faith* book and CD-ROM and in the *Sing-Along* video.

Activity: Hill Cumorah's Treasure

OBJECTIVE—To Learn About Prophets' Testimonies of Jesus in the Book of Mormon: Children will learn how prophets in the Book of Mormon testified of Jesus Christ's life and mission. They will also learn how this sacred record was hidden and found in the Hill Cumorah. They will learn why this sacred record was saved for our day. Read *More Lesson Ideas* #3 on the following page.

TO MAKE VISUALS: Copy, color, and cut out the *Hill Cumorah* story visuals, golden plates, and scripture trees. Mount the Hill Cumorah visual

on a poster and laminate the entire poster. Laminate other visuals, cut out, and place double-stick tape on backs. Mount trees on hill and story visuals (e.g., Moroni burying the golden plates, Joseph Smith finding the golden plates) as you talk about them (see #1 that follows).

ACTIVITY:

1. Show the visuals (shown above) and tell children about the Hill Cumorah's spiritual treasure (the golden plates) hidden in ancient America and found in the latter days, as follows on the next page. (Point to the empty box in the hill where the plates were buried and found.)

Ancient America: Just before the destruction of the Nephites, Mormon, a Nephite prophet, was commanded by the Lord to hide up sacred records written by prophets on golden plates. He and his son Moroni buried them in the Hill Cumorah so that the Lamanites would not destroy them (Mormon 6:2-11).

Latter Days: Fourteen hundred years later, that same Moroni appeared to Joseph Smith and told him where the plates were. Joseph Smith translated these plates into the Book of Mormon. The Book of Mormon is another testament of Jesus Christ. It tells about the people who lived in ancient America, and it contains the ancient prophets' testimonies of Jesus. These words were written hundreds of years ago, but they were written for our day to guide us. Let's learn about the treasures found in the golden plates: the scriptures known as the Book of Mormon.

2. *Scripture Search:* Ahead of time, mount trees on the Hill Cumorah. Have children take turns pulling up trees from the Hill Cumorah to find testaments of Jesus Christ (scriptures) from the ancient prophets in the Book of Mormon. They tell of His life and mission (Jacob 7:11). Divide the scriptures evenly between classes, and have the children take the scriptures to their class and look them up with their teacher. Then have the children present the scriptures one at a time to the group, saying how each scripture testifies of Jesus Christ.

3. *Scripture Chase:* Have older children compete in teams to race to find the scriptures. Award points to the team that finds the scripture first, and do #2 above to complete the activity. Children can also identify which prophet testified of Jesus Christ as follows:

NEPHI, SON OF LEHI - **2 Nephi 25:26,29**   ALMA - **Alma 7:13**   ALMA - **Alma 5:48**

NEPHI, SON OF HELAMAN - **3 Nephi 11:8-10**   MORMON - **3 Nephi 5:20**

HELAMAN, SON OF ALMA THE YOUNGER - **Helaman 5:12**   CAPTAIN MORONI - **Alma 44:4**

SAMUEL THE LAMANITE - **Helaman 14:11-12**   KING BENJAMIN - **Mosiah 4:11-12**

MORONI - **Mormon 9:21**   KING BENJAMIN - **Moses 3:17**   NEPHI, SON OF LEHI - **2 Nephi 25:13**

More Lesson Ideas (teach the theme using the concepts below and the above activity):

1. **The Lord restored the fulness of the gospel through Joseph Smith** (Acts 3:20-21; 2 Nephi 3:6-15; Joseph Smith—History 1:18-19, 26, 30, 33-34; "Apostasy" and "Restoration of the Gospel," *True to the Faith*, 13-14, 135-39).

2. **Joseph Smith translated the Book of Mormon by the power of God** (Joseph Smith—History 1:27-54; 59-67; *Primary 5*, lessons 5-7).

3. **The Book of Mormon is the word of God and is another testament of Jesus Christ** (D&C 19:26-27; Articles of Faith 1:8; title page of the Book of Mormon). In addition to the 2007 Primary outline, you may also use the following quote by Bishop Joseph L. Wirthlin: "By divine direction, this young man, Joseph Smith, unearthed a sacred record buried centuries ago in the ancient Hill Cumorah. This record contained the revelations of the Lord to the people that lived upon this the American Continent centuries ago. The scriptures in this holy record are among the most profound ever given to any people or in any dispensation" (Conference Report, April 1954, First Day—General Priesthood Meeting, 3).

4. **The priesthood was restored. A living prophet holds all the keys and authority of the priesthood and leads the Church under the direction of Jesus Christ** (Joseph Smith—History 1:68-72; D&C 27:12; "Follow the Prophet," *Children's Songbook*, 110-11; "Priesthood" and "Prophets," *True to the Faith*, 124-28, 129-30; *Gospel Principles*, chapters 13-14).

There4, 🐝+hold, 👁🍋 pro+🌱

2 do a marvellous work among this 👨‍👩‍👧‍👦, even a marvellous work and a 1+der.

Isaiah 29:14

Do not cut along the dotted line. Use this margin to mount the other side.

Hill Cumo

easure

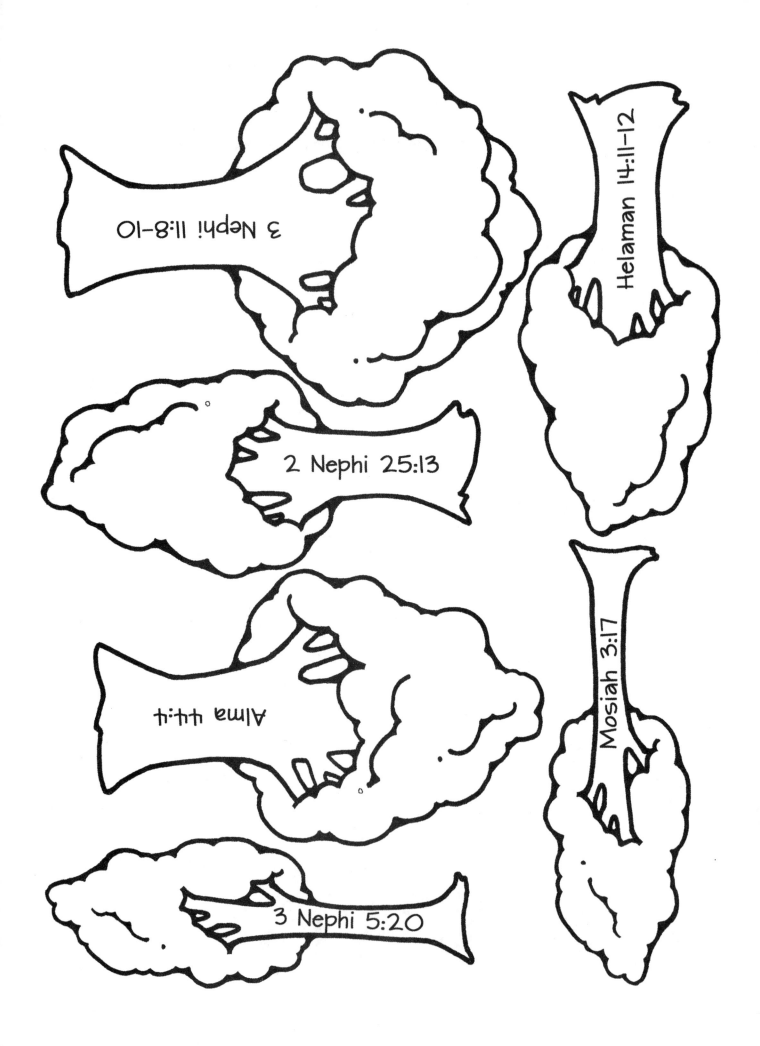

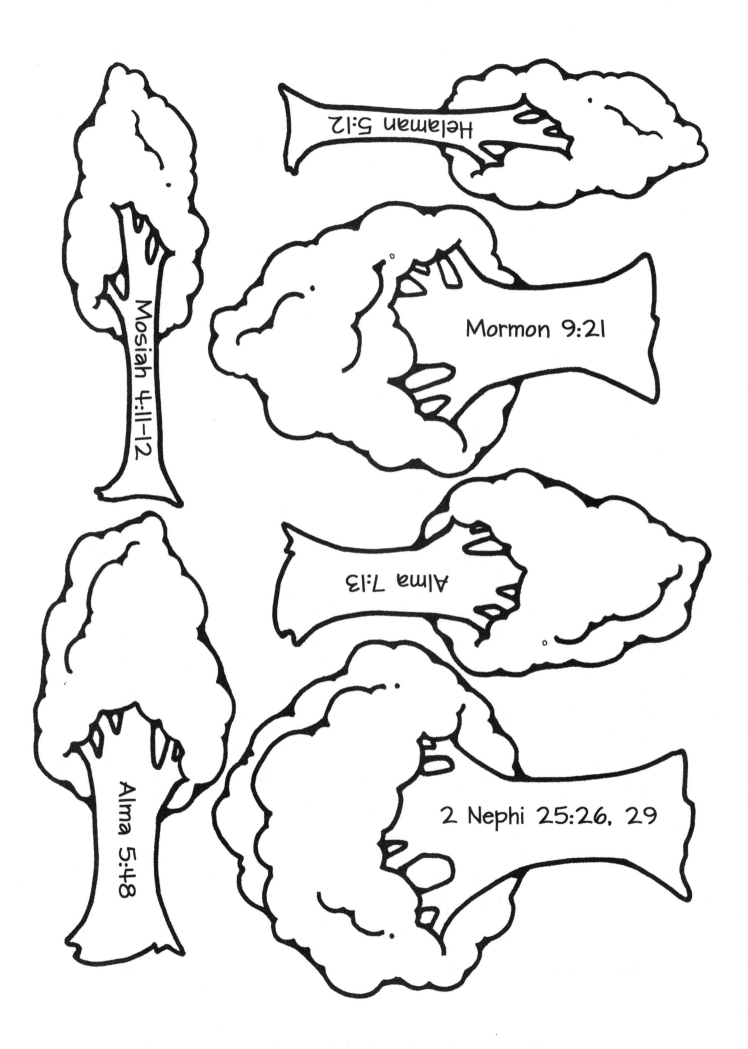

Theme 6   I Follow Jesus Christ in Faith
When I Make and Keep My Baptismal Covenant

Scripture to Memorize:

Memorize *John 3:5* using visual shown right.

Song:

Sing "I Want to Live the Gospel" in the *Children's Songbook*, 148. The song is illustrated in the *Primary Partners® Singing Fun!—I'll Follow Him in Faith* book and CD-ROM and in the *Sing-Along* video.

Activity: Baptism Promises Match Game

OBJECTIVE—To Remember Our Baptismal Promises: Children will learn how they can make and keep the same sacred covenants made by those baptized at the waters of Mormon (Mosiah 18:8-10). When we are baptized, we make promises to follow Jesus, and we renew these promises every week when we partake of the sacrament. Read *More Lesson Ideas* #1-2 on the following page.

TO MAKE VISUALS: Copy, color, and cut out the five covenant reminder pictures and reminder cards. Mount pictures on board and place cards in a container to draw from.

ACTIVITY:

1. Ahead of time, tie a string on each child's finger (teachers can help).

2. Say, "Sometimes we tie a string around our finger to help us remember something very important. When we are baptized we make special promises that are very important to us and to Heavenly Father. The prophet Alma in the Book of Mormon is talking to those who went to the waters of Mormon to be baptized. In Mosiah 18:8-10 we read about these special promises:

Step 1: 'As ye are desirous to come into the fold of God, and to be called his people, and are willing to BEAR one another's burdens, that they may be light (MOUNT PICTURE ON BOARD);

Step 2: Yea, and are willing to MOURN with those that mourn (MOUNT PICTURE);

Step 3: Yea, and COMFORT those that stand in need of comfort (MOUNT PICTURE),

Step 4: and to STAND as witnesses of God at all times and in all things, and in all places that ye may be in, even until death (MOUNT PICTURE), . . .

Step 5: that ye will serve him and KEEP his commandments (MOUNT PICTURE).'

Step 6: If we keep these five covenants or promises we make at baptism, God will 'pour out his Spirit more abundantly upon [us]' (REVIEW PICTURES)."

3. Ask children one at a time to draw a covenant reminder card, read it, and place it below the matching picture (to remind us of the covenants we made at baptism). *Note:* Pay attention to the letter on each card. When a child places the card on the board below the picture (as shown), the letter on the card should match with the first letter on each picture, e.g., the letter "B" on the card matches with "B" on the "Bear one another's burdens" picture.

More Lesson Ideas (teach the theme using the concepts below and the above activity):

1. **Jesus Christ was baptized** (Matthew 3:13-17; 2 Nephi 31:4-9; D&C 20:37; Articles of Faith 1:4; "Baptism," *Children's Songbook*, 100-101; *Gospel Principles*, chapters 18-20; Gospel Art Picture Kit [GAK], 208). You may also tell how Jesus kept these promises in His life, and refer to the following excerpts from the *New Testament Stories* (pages numbers in parentheses): "Jesus Brings Lazarus Back to Life" (102), for *Mourn with Those Who Mourn*, "Jesus is Tempted" (34), for *Keep the Commandments*; "The Sermon on the Mount" (48), for *Stand as a Witness*; "The Ten Lepers" (86), for *Comfort Those that Need Comfort*; and "Jesus Suffers in the Garden of Gethsemane" (111), for *Bear One Another's Burdens*.

2. **When I am baptized, I covenant with Heavenly Father that I will take upon myself the name of Jesus Christ, always remember Him, and keep His commandments** (D&C 20:77; "Baptism," *True to the Faith*, 21-26; "I Want to Live the Gospel," *Children's Songbook*, 148).

3. **After I am baptized, I will be confirmed a member of The Church of Jesus Christ of Latter-day Saints and receive the gift of the Holy Ghost** (3 Nephi 18:36-37; 4 Nephi 1:1; "The Gift of the Holy Ghost" and "Laying On of Hands," *True to the Faith*, 83-84, 95; GAK 601, 602; "The Church of Jesus Christ," *Children's Songbook*, 77).

4. **I partake of the sacrament to renew my baptismal covenant with Heavenly Father** (3 Nephi 18:7, 10-11; D&C 20:77, 79; "The Sacrament," *Children's Songbook*, 72; "Sacrament," *True to the Faith*, 147-149; *Gospel Principles*, chapter 23).

John 3:5

I will fast
and give money
to the poor.
(B)

I will earn money
to help pay for
my cousin's cancer
treatments.
(B)

I will write a
letter to a
soldier at war.
(B)

I will help
my sister do
her reading.
(B)

I will set the
table for Mother.
(B)

I will help my
grandpa walk
after his surgery.
(B)

I will help my
teacher correct
papers after school.
(B)

I will help my
father weed
the garden.
(B)

I will cry with
my brother because
his dog died.
(M)

I will let my dad
know I feel sad
he lost his job.
(M)

I will help make
a cake to take
to a funeral.
(M)

I will make a
card to send
to a widow who
lost her husband.
(M)

I will tell my aunt
how sad I felt
when her baby died.
(M)

I will listen to
Grandma's stories
about Grandpa
when he was alive.
(M)

I will visit an
older neighbor whose
wife has just died.
(M)

I will help Mom
pick flowers
to put on
Grandpa's grave.
(M)

I will send a
care package to
a missionary
serving far away.
(C)

I will take
puzzles and books
to a friend with
a broken leg.
(C)

I will get my dad
an ice pack for
his sore back.
(C)

I will smile and
tell a joke to cheer
up a sad friend.
(C)

I will hold my
little brother who
stubbed his toe.
(C)

I will make a
get-well card
for a sick friend.
(C)

I will ask a sad
boy at school if
he wants to play.
(C)

I will take
some cookies to
a neighbor
who is lonely.
(C)

I will learn
important
scriptures.
(S)

I will be an
example
for others.
(S)

I will bear my
testimony that the
gospel is true.
(S)

I will tell others
that we are all
God's children.
(S)

I will give a
Book of Mormon
to a friend.
(S)

I will tell others
about the gospel
of Jesus Christ.
(S)

I will invite a
friend to Primary.
(S)

I will learn to
be a missionary.
(S)

I will keep the
Word of Wisdom.

(K)

I will pay
my tithing.

(K)

I will use
clean language.

(K)

I will go
to church.

(K)

I will have family
home evening.

(K)

I will be honest
in all I do
and say.

(K)

I will keep the
Sabbath day holy.

(K)

I will listen
to and obey
my parents.

(K)

Theme 7   My Family Can Follow
Jesus Christ in Faith

Scripture to Memorize:

Memorize *The Family: A Proclamation to the World,* paragraph 7, using visual shown right.

Activity: "Honorable Family" Food Storage Match

OBJECTIVE—To Show Faith Through Obedience, Respect, and Love: Help children ponder family situations that invite honoring and obeying parents or showing respect for others, and doing as Jesus would do. Read *More Lesson Ideas* #3-4 on the following page.

Bite-size Memorize

☺+ness in life is most likely 2 🐝 achieved when founded 🆙on the teachings of the Lord 🧔

The Family: A Proclamation to the World Paragraph 7

TO MAKE VISUALS: Copy, color, and cut out the food storage situation cards and cupboard that follow and cut cards in half where indicated. Laminate for durability. Laminate one or two posters to mount cupboard and cards on.

ACTIVITY: Tell children that Jesus honored His mother, Mary. When He was about to die on the cross in much pain, He still thought of His mother, asking John to take care of her (John 19:25-27). We need to love and care for our family. Our prophet, Gordon B. Hinckley, tells us to "love each other, respect each other, to treat each other with love, kindness, and respect" *(Teachings of Gordon B. Hinckley,* 25).

1. Place the *Honorable Family Food Storage* cupboard in the center of poster. Read and show the match cards, putting them together and listing the ways these family members honored and showed respect for their family. Explain that they did as Jesus would do to make a happy home.

2. Divide the cards in half, placing the left half of the cards (e.g., "Tommy Tomato helped his brother study . . .") on the left side of the board, and placing the right half of the cards (e.g., "and catch up on his homework") on the right side of the board.

3. Have children take turns choosing a left-side card and matching it with a right-side card and then placing it in the cupboard (mounting with tape).

4. Talk about each action (and others that children want to share) that helps show honor and respect to our family, to do as Jesus would do.

More Lesson Ideas (teach the theme using the concepts below and the above activity):

1. **I can learn about righteous families by reading the scriptures** (Moses 5:1-2, 5, 10-12, 58; 6:1; Luke 2:1-16; Matthew 9:18-19, 23-25; Mark 5:22-24, 35-43; Luke 8:41-42, 49-56; 1 Nephi 2:1-7; Mosiah 27; Alma 53:10-21; 56:44-56; 58:39).

2. **The first member of my family to join the Church followed Jesus in faith. I can learn about my family history** (D&C 136:2, 4, 11; "To Be a Pioneer," *Children's Songbook,* 218-19; "Family History Work and Genealogy," *True to the Faith,* 61-64).

3. **I will honor my father and mother and show respect for others in my family** (Exodus 20:12; "Case Studies" and "Puppets," *Teaching, No Greater Call,* 161-62, 176-77).

4. **My family can follow Jesus Christ in faith by holding family prayer, family scripture study, and family home evening** ("Family Prayer," "Love Is Spoken Here," and "Family Night," *Children's Songbook,* 189, 190-191, 195; "Family Home Evening," "Family Prayer," and "Importance of Daily Scripture Study," *True to the Faith,* 65-66, 122, 155-56).

🙂+ness in life is most likely 2 🐝 achieved when founded UPon the teachings of the Lord

Jesus Christ

The Family: A Proclamation to the World
Paragraph 7

Susie
SUGAR
sweet and refined!

was sweet on family prayer...

...and gathered her family each night to pray.

Hayley
Honey
helps her brother out of a sticky situation...

...by showing him how to choose the right.

FRED
FLOUR
sifts through his scriptures to find a lesson...

...he can give for family home evening.

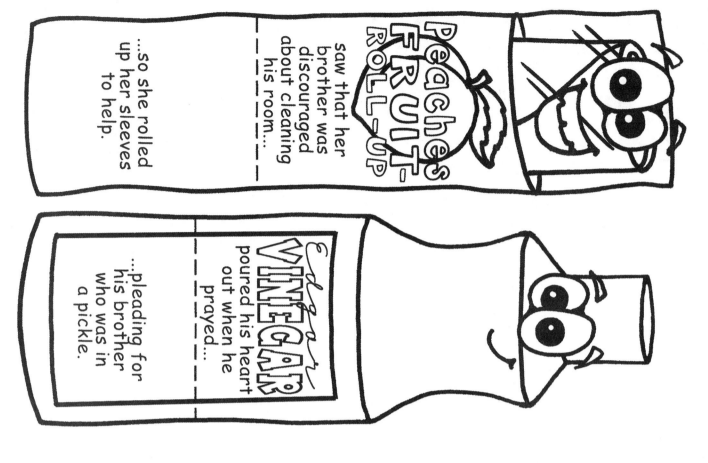

Peaches FRUIT ROLL-UP

saw that her brother was discouraged about cleaning his room...

...so she rolled up her sleeves to help.

Edgar VINEGAR

poured his heart out when he prayed...

...pleading for his brother who was in a pickle.

Meg Nutmeg

liked to hear laughter in the home...

...so she made up fun games to spice things up.

Sissy SOUP

was a "soup"er sport when her brother yelled at her...

...because she didn't yell back or stew about it.

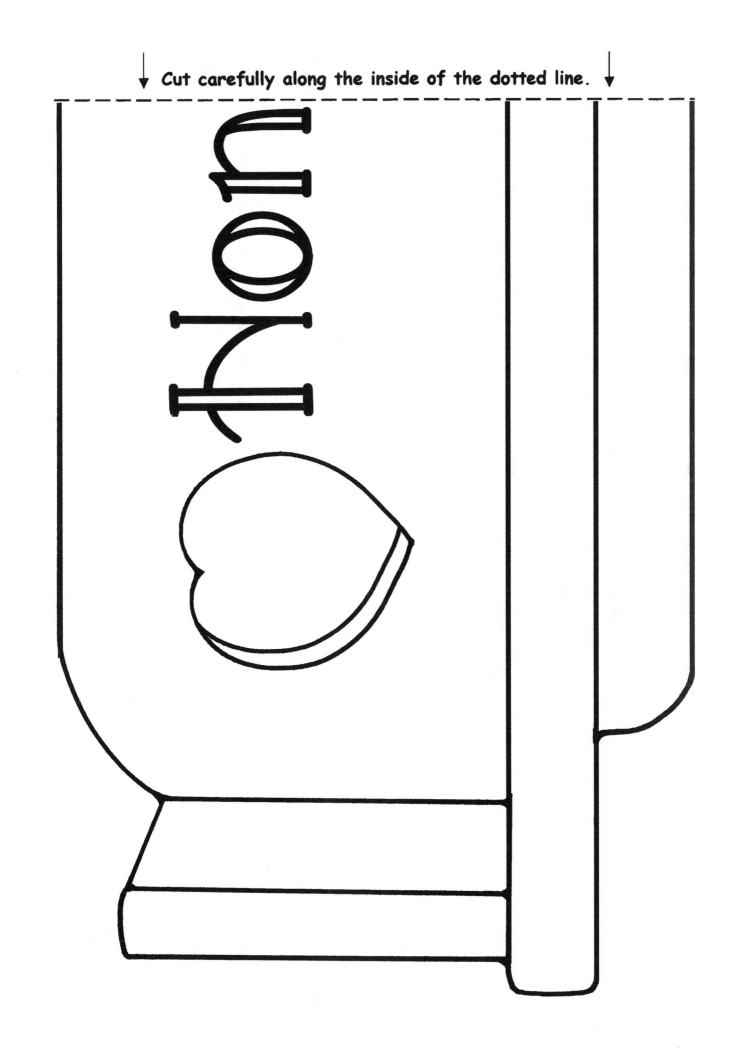

Orable Food Storage

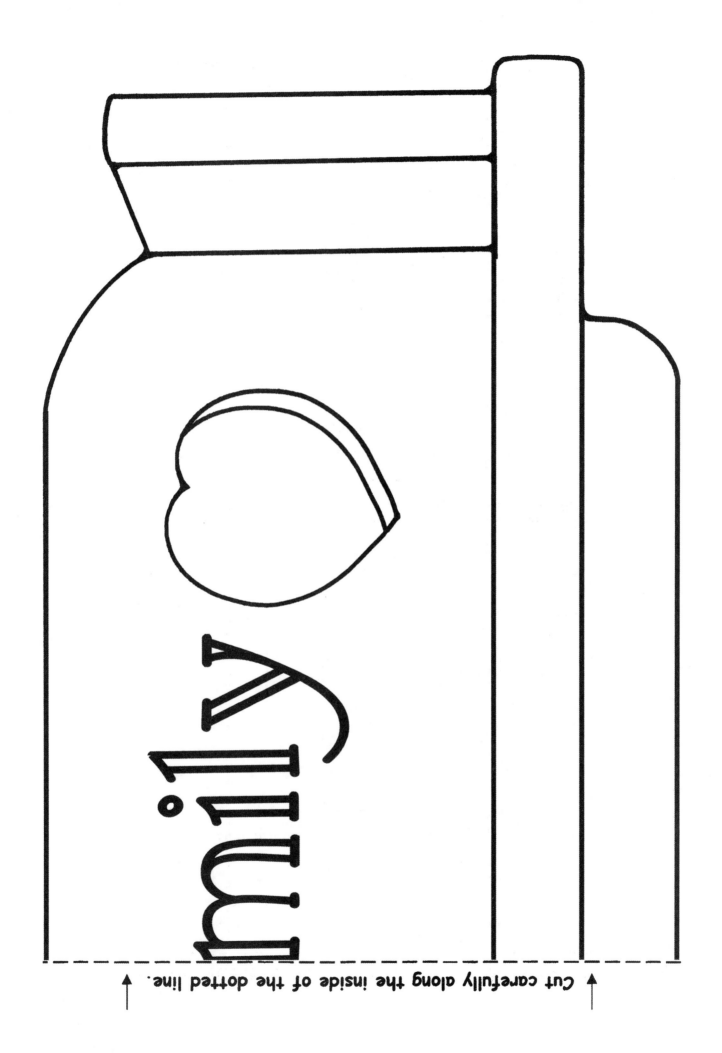

Theme 8   My Faith in Jesus Christ Grows When I Listen to the Holy Ghost

Bite-size Memorize

4. @+hold, the Comforter knoweth all things, and @eth ⦿ of the @ Father and of the ☼.

D&C 42:17

Scripture to Memorize:

Memorize *D&C 42:17* using visual shown right.

Activity: Gifts of Testimony Exchange

OBJECTIVE—To Listen to the Holy Ghost: Children will learn five truths that we can receive from the Holy Ghost as He speaks to our mind and heart, and five things we can do in exchange to receive these gifts of testimony. Read *More Lesson Ideas* #1 on the following page.

TO MAKE VISUALS: Copy, color, and cut out the five gift boxes and gift-exchange hearts that follow. Laminate visuals and cut out again. Fold boxes and glue or tape together, leaving the top open to insert hearts. Insert hearts in the right box (see *ANSWERS* on the following page).

EXPLAIN THE GODHEAD:

Tell about the Holy Ghost as a member of the Godhead as follows:

1. Heavenly Father is a member of the Godhead. He is God, the Eternal Father, the father of our spirits.

2. Jesus Christ is a member of the Godhead. He is Heavenly Father's Only Begotten Son who was sent to earth to show us how to live. Jesus is our Heavenly Brother.

3. Heavenly Father and Jesus have bodies of flesh and bones and created us to be like Them.

4. Heavenly Father and Jesus created the earth on which we live and sent us here to live Heavenly Father's plan.

5. The Holy Ghost is a member of the Godhead, but He does not have a body of flesh and bones. He is a personage of spirit. This way He can dwell in our mind and in our heart. His purpose is to tell us what Heavenly Father and Jesus want us to know so we can follow Heavenly Father's plan and return to our heavenly home someday.

GIFT EXCHANGE ACTIVITY:

Scriptures to Review:

 • D&C 8:2, "Yea, behold, I will tell you in your mind and in your heart, by the Holy Ghost, which shall come upon you and which shall dwell in your heart."

 • The Holy Ghost loves us and wants us to have a testimony (a special witness) of five important things. They come from Him to our heart. Review testimony gifts.

 • If we want these gifts we must earn them.

1. On a table, display the five boxes that represent gifts of testimony from the Holy Ghost, and read and talk about each.

2. Tell children, "The Holy Ghost can give us gifts of testimony, but we must earn these gifts in exchange by giving—by doing our part to receive those gifts." Ask children to take turns coming up and pulling a heart from the box. Each heart represents a heartfelt gift we can give in exchange. E.g., to receive the gift of testimony that "God is our Father in Heaven," we can (shown on hearts): keep His commandments, pray to Him, receive guidance from Him through the Holy Ghost.

3. After each heart is pulled from the box, place it in a container to draw from. If time allows, have children take turns drawing a heart and placing it in the right box.

ANSWERS: *Five Gifts of Testimony from the Holy Ghost and Five Heartfelt Gifts We Can Give in Exchange:*

1. God is our Father in Heaven: keep His commandments, pray to Him, receive guidance from Him.

2. Jesus Christ is Heavenly Father's Son and is our Savior and Redeemer: study His life in the scriptures, follow His example, remember Him during the sacrament.

3. The Book of Mormon was translated by the power of God by Joseph Smith, who is a prophet of God: read this book, pray about this book (Moroni 10:3-5), ponder its message.

4. The Church of Jesus Christ of Latter-day Saints is the Lord's true Church: attend church to learn the gospel, live the gospel principles, pray to know the Church is true.

5. We have a living prophet on the earth today: read and listen to his words in general conference, pray to know he is a prophet of God, live his latter-day teachings.

More Lesson Ideas (teach the theme using the concepts below and the above activity):

1. **A testimony is a spiritual witness given by the Holy Ghost** (3 Nephi 28:11; Moroni 10:4-5; "The Spirit Is the True Teacher," *Teaching, No Greater Call*, 41-42; *Primary 5*, lesson 46; "Testimony," *True to the Faith*, 178-80).

2. **I invite the promptings of the Holy Ghost when I pray, read the scriptures, keep the commandments, and follow the living prophets** (Alma 5:45-46; D&C 6:14-15; 138:1, 6, 11; Carlos E. Asay, "Courting the Holy Ghost," *Friend*, Aug. 1991, inside front cover).

3. **I can recognize the promptings of the Holy Ghost** (Romans 15:13; "Recognizing and Following the Spirit in Your Teaching," *Teaching, No Greater Call*, 47-48). Share scriptures that teach about the promptings of the Holy Ghost: Moroni 8:25-26; Galatians 5:22-23; D&C 36:2; John 14:26; D&C 8:2; and D&C 9:7-9. Bear testimony of the Holy Ghost. Sing "I Know My Father Lives," *Children's Songbook*, 5.

4. **The Holy Ghost testifies of Jesus Christ and can teach, guide, warn, protect, and comfort me** (John 14:26; 15:26; 2 Nephi 31:17; Moroni 10:5; D&C 6:14-15; 8:2; 11:12; 20:27; "The Still Small Voice," *Children's Songbook*, 106-7; "Roles of the Holy Ghost," *True to the Faith*, 82).

4, 🐝+hold, the Comforter knoweth all things, and 🧸+eth 💿 of the Father and of the ☀️.

D&C 42:17

Glue bow here.

Jesus Christ is Heavenly
Father's Son and is
our Savior and Redeemer.

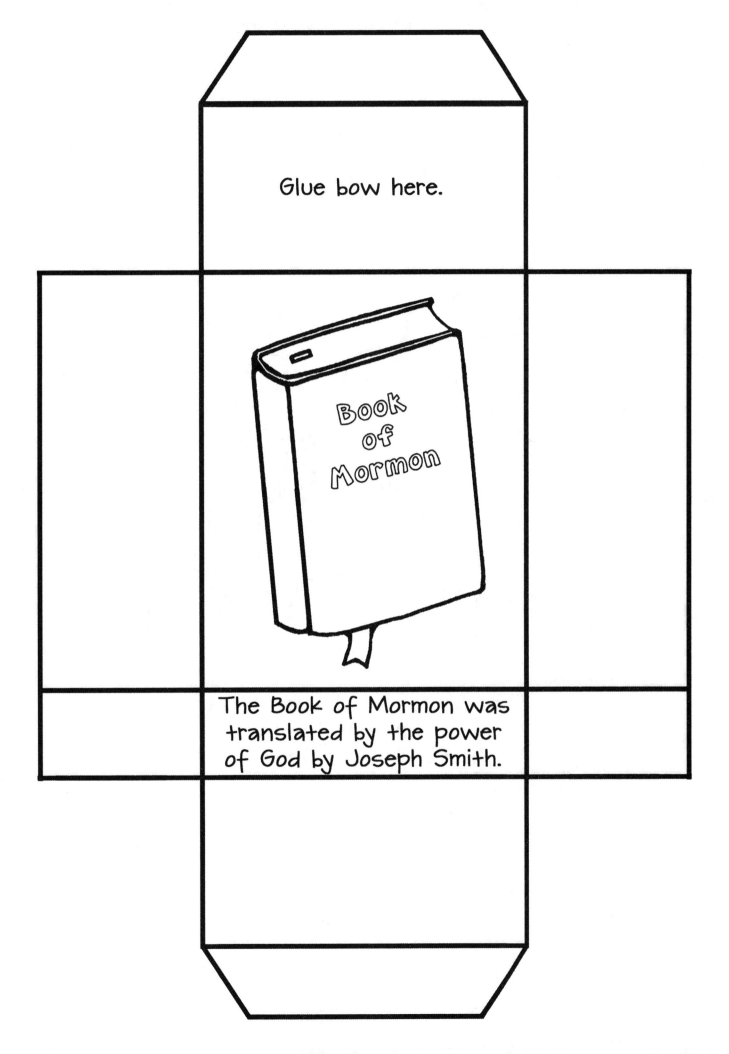

Glue bow here.

Book
of
Mormon

The Book of Mormon was translated by the power of God by Joseph Smith.

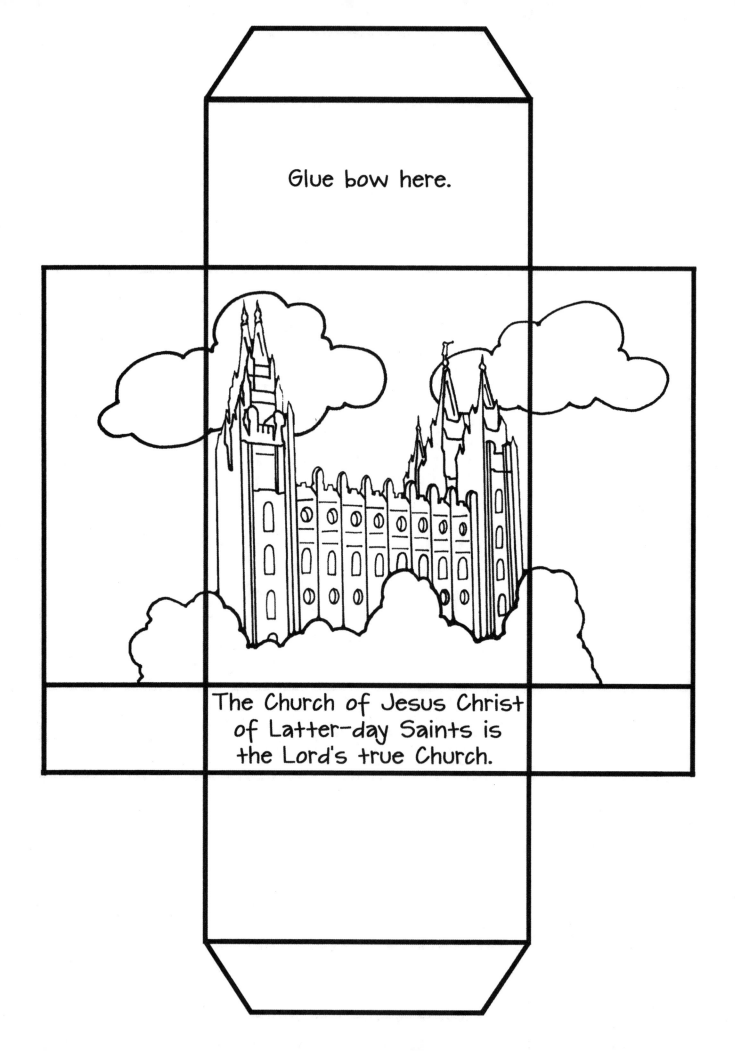

Glue bow here.

The Church of Jesus Christ of Latter-day Saints is the Lord's true Church.

Glue bow here.

We have a living prophet
on the earth today.

Make 5 copies.

Back
Fold

Front
Fold

Back
Fold

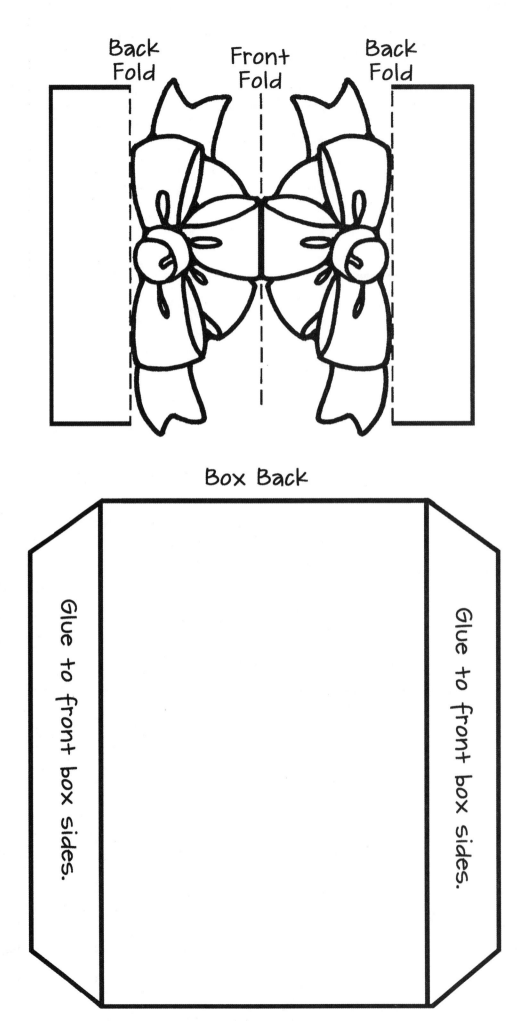

Box Back

Glue to front box sides.

Glue to front box sides.

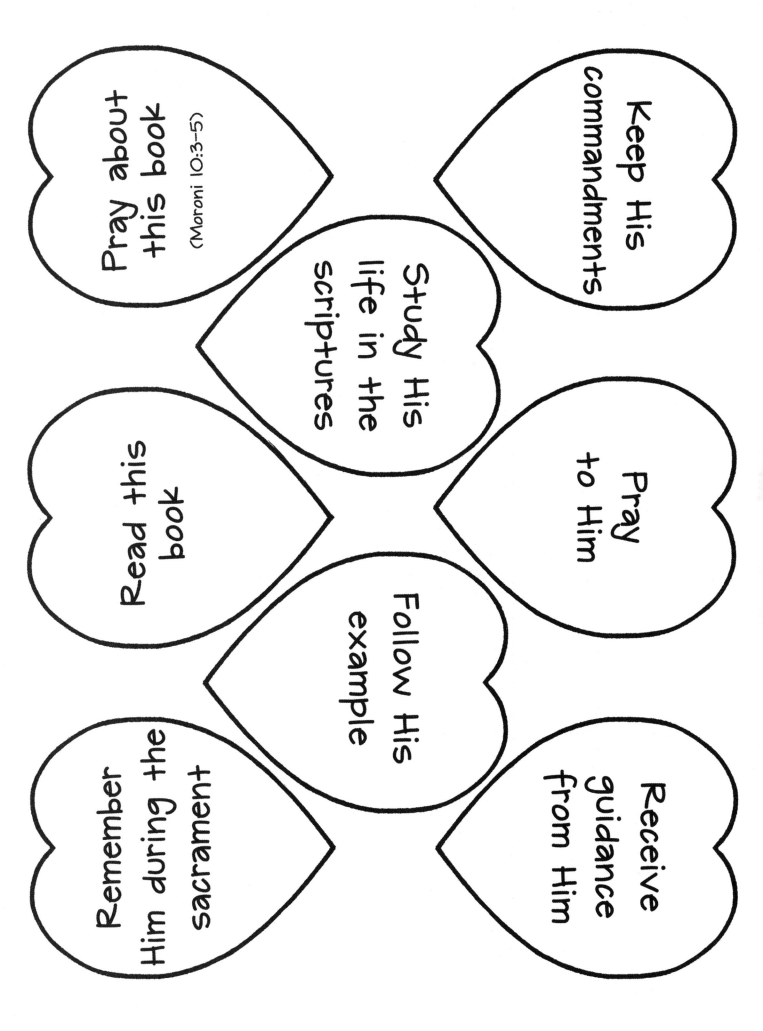

Pray about this book (Moroni 10:3-5)

Keep His commandments

Study His life in the scriptures

Read this book

Pray to Him

Follow His example

Remember Him during the sacrament

Receive guidance from Him

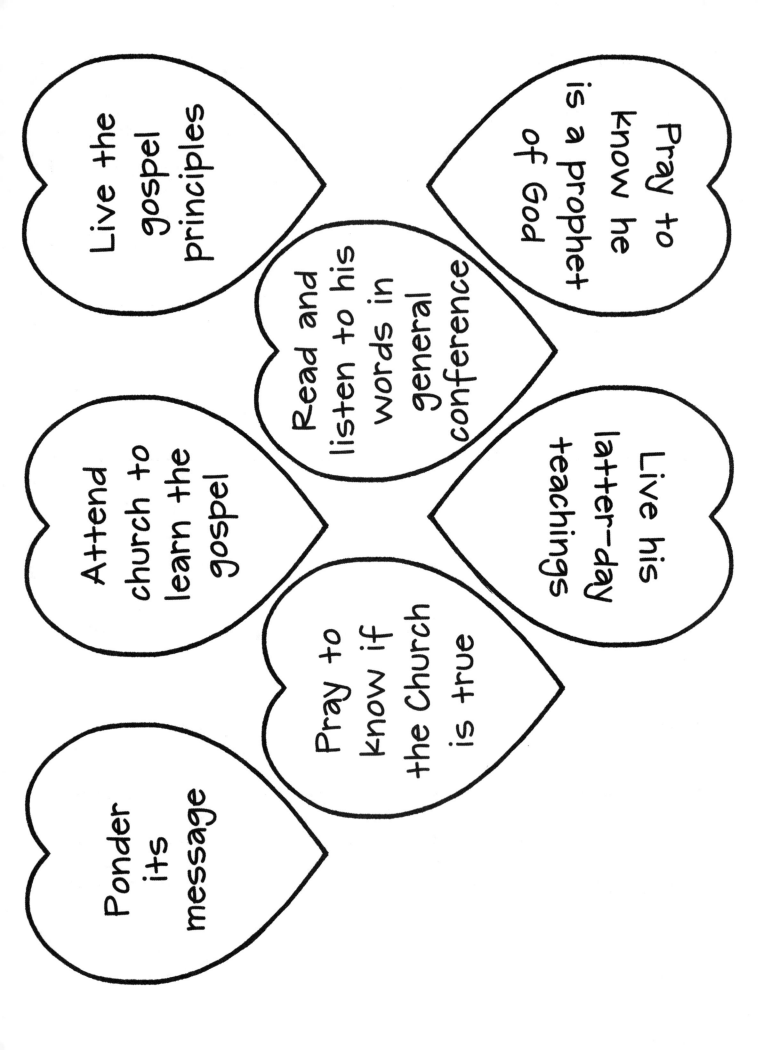

Theme 9   My Faith in Jesus Christ Grows When I Serve Others

Scripture to Memorize:

Memorize *Mosiah 2:17* using visual shown right.

Activity: Service Road Game

OBJECTIVE—To Be Like Jesus by Serving Others: Children will learn how Jesus was of service and how they can be of service today. Read *More Lesson Ideas #1-4* on the following page.

TO MAKE VISUALS: Copy, color, and cut out the *Service Road* parts A-D, die-block, and feet markers. Glue *Service Road* parts together. Fold die and tabs, and glue where indicated to create block. When coloring feet markers, color sandals different colors (to specify teams).

Bite-size Memorize

When ye R in the service of UR fellow 🐝+ings ye R only in the service of UR God.

Mosiah 2:17

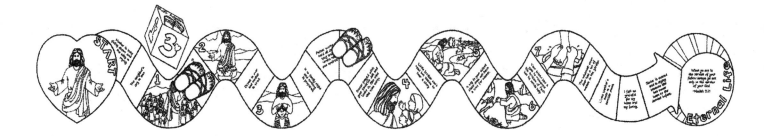

ACTIVITY:

1. Ahead of time, assign different *Jesus Service Stories #1-7* to classes to read aloud when their number is called.

2. Post the *Service Road* and tell children, "Our faith in Jesus Christ grows as we learn how He served others and as we look for ways we can serve. When we serve others we are serving Jesus (review *Bite-size Memorize* for this lesson). If we have a life of service we can become like Jesus. Then we—like Jesus—can have eternal life, to live with Heavenly Father again someday."

3. Divide children into two teams and have children take turns rolling the die-block and moving the team's feet marker forward from the START position, according to the number on the die.

4. If a player moves to the "Jesus Story" position on the board, read the number aloud. Have the class member who has that story number present the story and tell how we can serve like Jesus. *Note:* If the second team that follows lands on the same story, have them paraphrase the story that was told or have the class read the story again. If they can tell the story because they listened well, give them a chance to play again.

5. If a player moves to a situation position on the board, have them read the situation and tell how they can serve.

6. Move to ETERNAL LIFE, and repeat game until time is up. If a team lands on a "Jesus Story" or situation they have landed on before, have them move to the next one. The first team to get to ETERNAL LIFE wins.

More Lesson Ideas (teach the theme using the concepts below and the above activity):

1. **Jesus Christ taught us to serve others** ("Service," *True to the Faith*, 161-62; *Gospel Principles*, chapter 28).
2. **I will serve in my family** (1 Nephi 16:17-32).
3. **I will serve others by treating them kindly and sharing what I have** (Luke 10:30-36; John 13:34-35; Galatians 5:13-14; "Kindness Begins with Me," *Children's Songbook*, 145).
4. **As I serve others, I serve Jesus Christ and show my love for Him** (Matthew 25:34-40; John 21:15-17; Mosiah 2:17-18; "Love One Another," *Children's Songbook*, 136).

When ye R in the service of UR fellow 🐝+ings ye R only in the service of UR God.

Mosiah 2:17

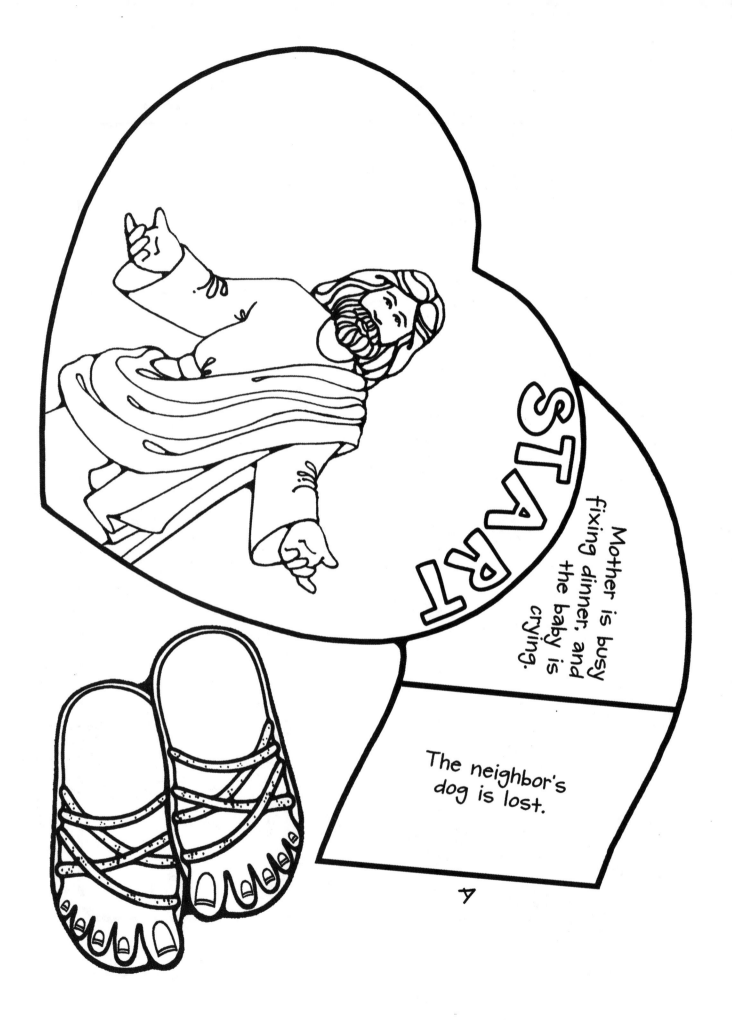

START

Mother is busy fixing dinner, and the baby is crying.

The neighbor's dog is lost.

A

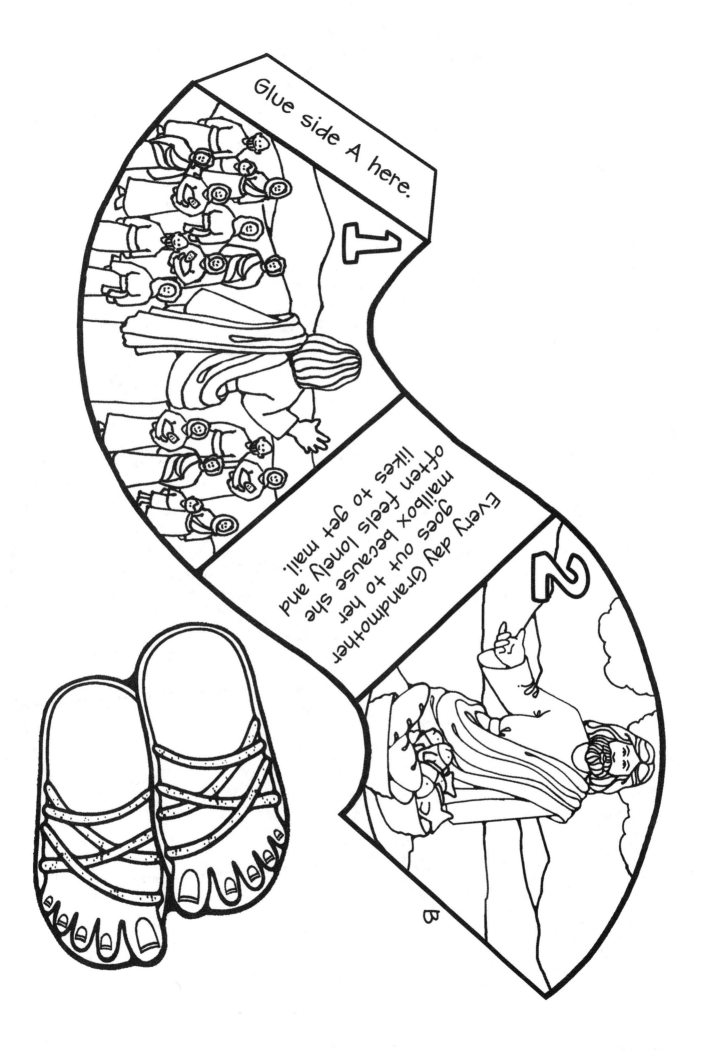

Glue side A here.

1

2

B

Every day Grandmother goes out to her mailbox because she often feels lonely and likes to get mail!

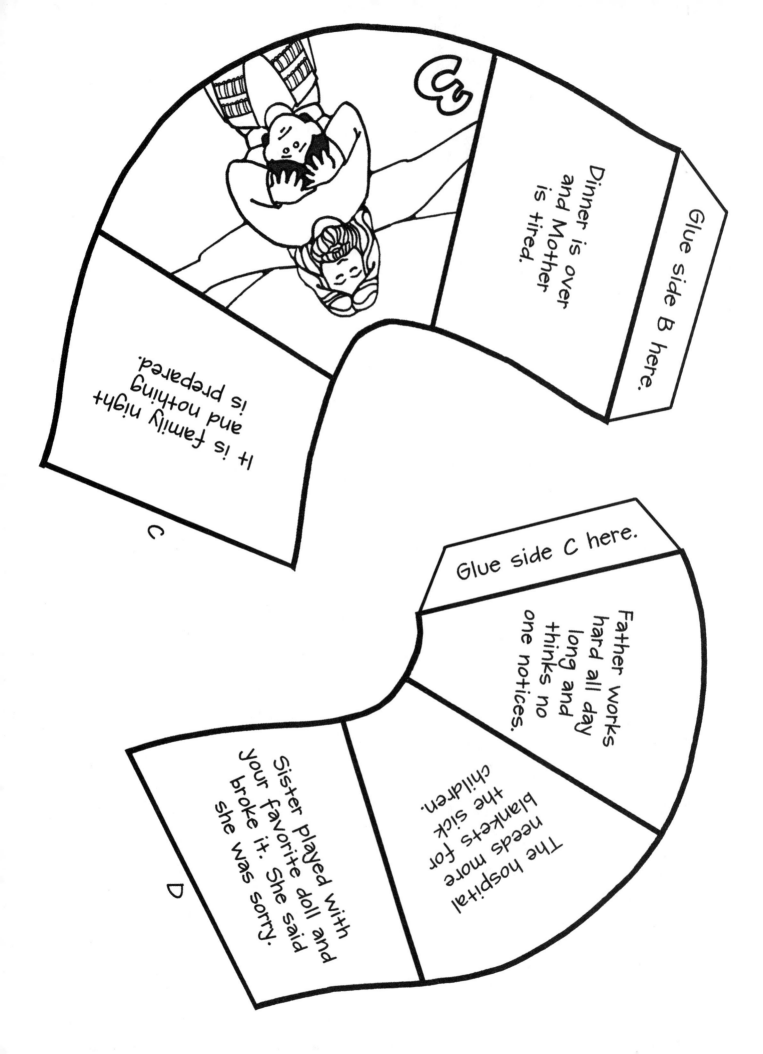

Glue side B here.

Dinner is over and Mother is tired.

It is family night and nothing is prepared.

C

3

Glue side C here.

Father works hard all day long and thinks no one notices.

The hospital needs more blankets for the sick children.

Sister played with your favorite doll and broke it. She said she was sorry.

D

Glue side D here.

4

Little brother can't read but wants to hear a story.

5

A boy in your school class does not have a coat for winter.

E

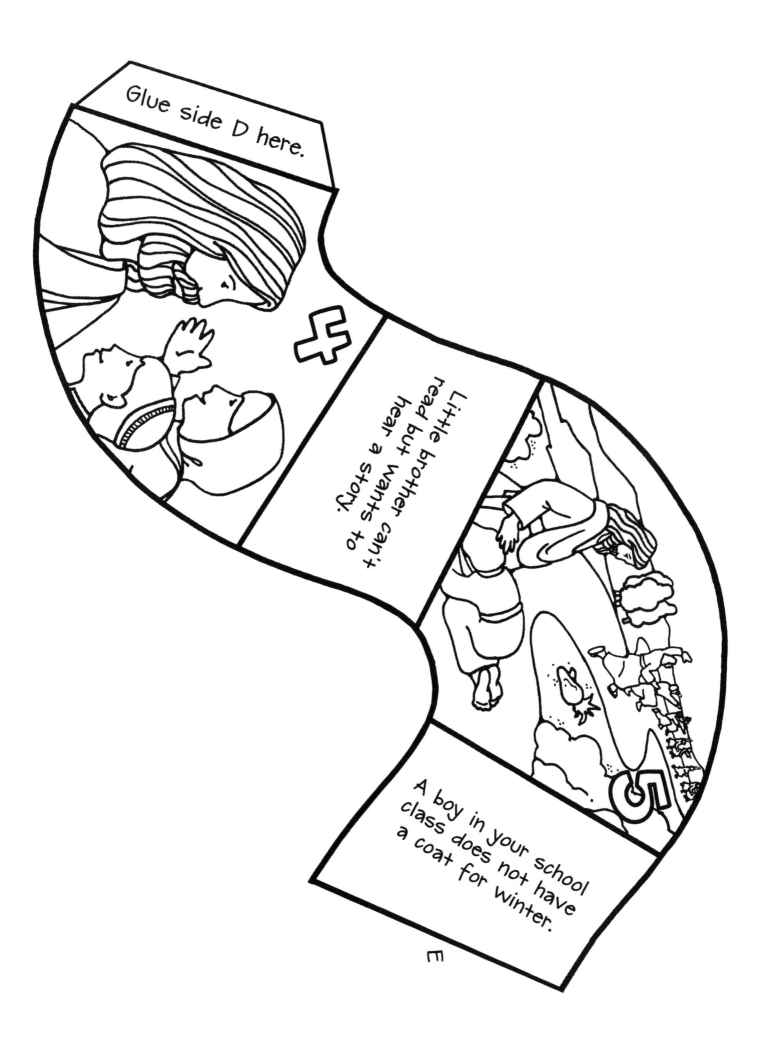

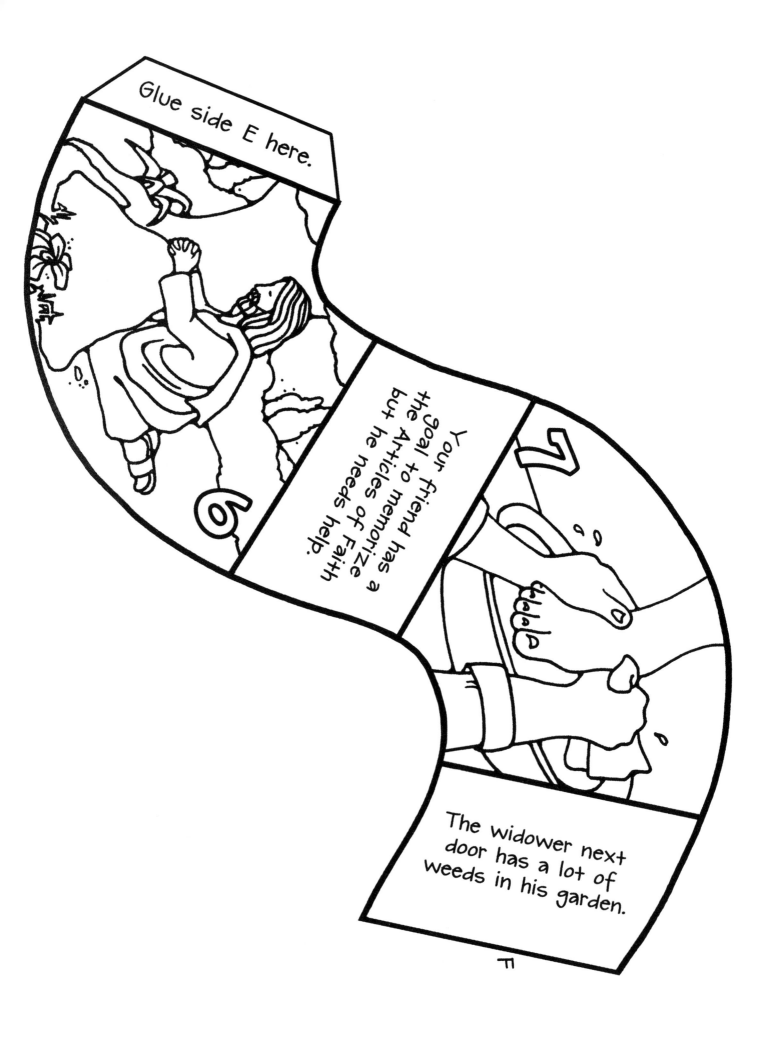

Glue side E here.

6

7

Your friend has a goal to memorize the Articles of Faith but he needs help.

The widower next door has a lot of weeds in his garden.

Glue side G here.

I feel so
grateful
for my
home and
my family.

Little brother's
room is a
horrible mess.

Glue side F here.

G

Sister is scared
and is crying
because she
has never
been to the
dentist before.

When ye are in
the service of your
fellow beings ye are
only in the service
of your God.
-Mosiah 2:17

Eternal Life

Jesus Service Stories

#1 Sermon on the Mount

Jesus went up on a high mountain, and thousands of people gathered to hear Him. He taught them the Beatitudes so they could learn to be happy. He taught them to be kind, to forgive, and to love others. He taught them how they can go back to heaven.
LIKE JESUS, WE SHOULD NOT BE AFRAID TO TELL OTHERS ABOUT THE GOSPEL.

#2 Jesus Feeds 5,000

When Jesus was teaching thousands of people on the mountain, He taught them all day until it was night. The people wanted to stay to hear more, but they were also hungry and had not brought food. Jesus told His disciples to go look for food. They only found five loaves of bread and two fish—not enough to feed 5,000. So, Jesus blessed the bread and fish and broke it into pieces. The disciples took the people food and there was more than enough to feed all of them; this was a miracle.
LIKE JESUS, WE CAN CARE ENOUGH AND SHARE OUR FOOD WITH THOSE IN NEED.

#3 Jesus Heals a Blind Man

One day Jesus was walking with His disciples, and they saw a blind man. His disciples thought the man was born blind because he or his parents had sinned. Jesus said they had not sinned. He said the man was born blind so that Jesus could heal him and show God's power. Jesus had a special power from God called the priesthood. He made mud out of dirt and put it on the man's eyes. Jesus told him to wash his eyes. When the man obeyed he could see. The man had faith and was healed.
LIKE JESUS, WE CAN HELP THE SICK.

#4 Jesus Heals Ten Lepers

Jesus went to a small town, where he saw ten men who were lepers. They had sores all over their bodies and their skin was falling off. Doctors could not help them, and people would not go near them or they would get sick too. The lepers asked Jesus to heal them, to make their sores go away. Jesus listened to them, and He wanted them to get well. He told them to go to the priests, and they obeyed. On the way to the priests, their sores disappeared; Jesus had healed them. One man came back, knelt down, and thanked Jesus for healing him.
LIKE JESUS, WE CAN CARE FOR OTHERS. LIKE THE ONE LEPER WHO GAVE THANKS, WE CAN GIVE THANKS TO JESUS AND OTHERS.

#5 Jesus Blesses the Children

One day Jesus was with His disciples and He was very tired. Some people wanted Jesus to bless their children, and the disciples told them not to bring them to Jesus. Jesus told His disciples to bring the children to Him. He told them they should love little children and they should have faith like little children. Jesus took the time to bless the children, and the children loved Jesus very much.

LIKE JESUS, WE CAN LOVE AND CARE FOR OTHERS, ESPECIALLY CHILDREN AND THE ELDERLY.

#6 Jesus Suffers in the Garden

At the end of His mission, Jesus went to the Garden of Gethsemane with His Apostles. He asked most of them to wait, but he asked three to come with Him while He went to pray. The three went to sleep because Jesus prayed for a very long time. Jesus came back and asked them to stay awake. Jesus prayed and was very sad. He began to shake and blood came out of His skin. His body hurt as He suffered for all of the sins of all people. Angels came to help make Him stronger. Jesus did not want to suffer, but He knew this must be done to obey Heavenly Father.

LIKE JESUS, WE CAN OBEY ALL OF HEAVENLY FATHER'S COMMANDMENTS.

#7 Jesus Washes His Apostles Feet

Jesus and His Apostles wore sandals instead of shoes. One day they came back very tired from walking, and their feet were sore and dirty. Jesus filled a bowl with water and wanted to wash Peter's feet. Peter said he did not want Jesus to wash his feet. Jesus said that if He could not wash Peter's feet, Peter could not be a "part" of Jesus. Peter then said he wanted Jesus to wash his feet, because he wanted to be His friend.

LIKE JESUS, WE CAN SERVE OTHERS, SHOWING OUR LOVE.

Theme 10   I Show My Faith in Jesus Christ
When I Share the Gospel with Others

Scripture to Memorize:

Memorize *Matthew 5:16* using visual shown right.

Activity: Blooming Good Example Garden

OBJECTIVE—To Learn Gospel Standards: Children will learn some of the gospel standards Jesus taught. They will also learn how we can blossom and grow and teach others about the gospel of Jesus Christ through our examples. Read *More Lesson Ideas* #1-4 on the following page and "My Gospel Standards" in the *Faith in God* booklet.

TO MAKE VISUALS: Copy, color, and cut out the *Gospel Standards* pots, stems, flower-child faces, and

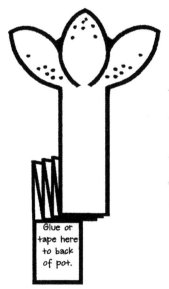

leaf action that follow. Laminate visuals and cut out again. Then fan-fold the stems where indicated, and glue or tape where indicated on the back of the pot (as shown on right). Loosely tape the pots on two laminated poster boards (on the sides and bottom of pots) so the fanfold won't be obstructed as it moves up and down. Place leaf action in a container to draw from. (You will need tape.)

Pull Up

99

The flower pots contain the following text:

I will only read and watch things that are pleasing to Heavenly Father.

I will keep my mind and body sacred and pure, and I will not partake of things that are harmful to me.

I will do those things on the Sabbath that will help me feel close to Heavenly Father and Jesus Christ.

I will honor my parents and do my part to strengthen my family.

I will use the names of Heavenly Father and Jesus Christ reverently. I will not swear or use crude words.

I will be honest with Heavenly Father, others, and myself.

I will seek good friends and treat others kindly.

ACTIVITY: Tell children that by living the gospel standards we can blossom and grow and help others by our examples. This way we are being missionaries. When they see our good examples, others will want to know more about the gospel. Let's learn how we can grow from living the gospel standards.

1. Review 7 of the 13 gospel standards written on the flower pots. Talk about each one. For younger children, you may want to reduce the number of gospel standards.

2. Move one of the stems up to show how we can grow in the gospel by living the gospel standards. Then place a head on the stem to show we are a "blooming good example" to others.

3. Divide children into two teams and have them take turns coming up and drawing a leaf action from a container, reading it aloud, and placing the leaf on the stem where the matching gospel standard is found. To attach a leaf, pull up stem one notch and tape to stem.

4. Repeat process until the third stem is up. Then have the last child choose a flower head to place on top to symbolize that we are a "blooming good example" to others.

More Lesson Ideas (teach the theme using the concepts below and the above activity):

1. **I will be a good example to others by the way I live** (1 Timothy 4:12; Alma 17:11; 53:20-21; "The Things I Do," *Children's Songbook*, 170-71).

2. **My testimony grows when I share it with my friends and hear the testimonies of others** (Mosiah 18:6-9; Alma 22:13-18; "We'll Bring the World His Truth," *Children's Songbook*, 172-73.)

3. **I will invite my friends to Primary** (D&C 4; "I will seek good friends and treat others kindly" in "My Gospel Standards"; "Kindness Begins with Me," *Children's Songbook*, 145; "Role Playing," *Teaching, No Greater Call*, 178).

4. **I will prepare now to become a missionary** (1 Timothy 4:12; David A Bednar, "Becoming a Missionary," *Ensign*, Nov. 2005, 44-47; "Basic Requirements" in "Faith in God Award Requirements," *Faith in God* guidebooks, 4-5).

Bite-size Memorize

Let UR 💡 so shine 🐝+4 👦👦, t+🪐 they may 👁️👁️ UR good works, and glorify UR Father which is in ☁️.

Matthew 5:16

I will use the names of Heavenly Father and Jesus Christ reverently. I will not swear or use crude words.

I will be honest with Heavenly Father, others, and myself.

I will honor my parents and do my part to strengthen my family.

I will do those things on the Sabbath that will help me feel close to Heavenly Father and Jesus Christ.

I will only read
and watch
things that
are pleasing
to Heavenly
Father.

- - - - - -

I will keep my
mind and body
sacred and pure,
and I will not
partake of
things that are
harmful to me.

- - - - - -

I will seek good friends and treat others kindly.

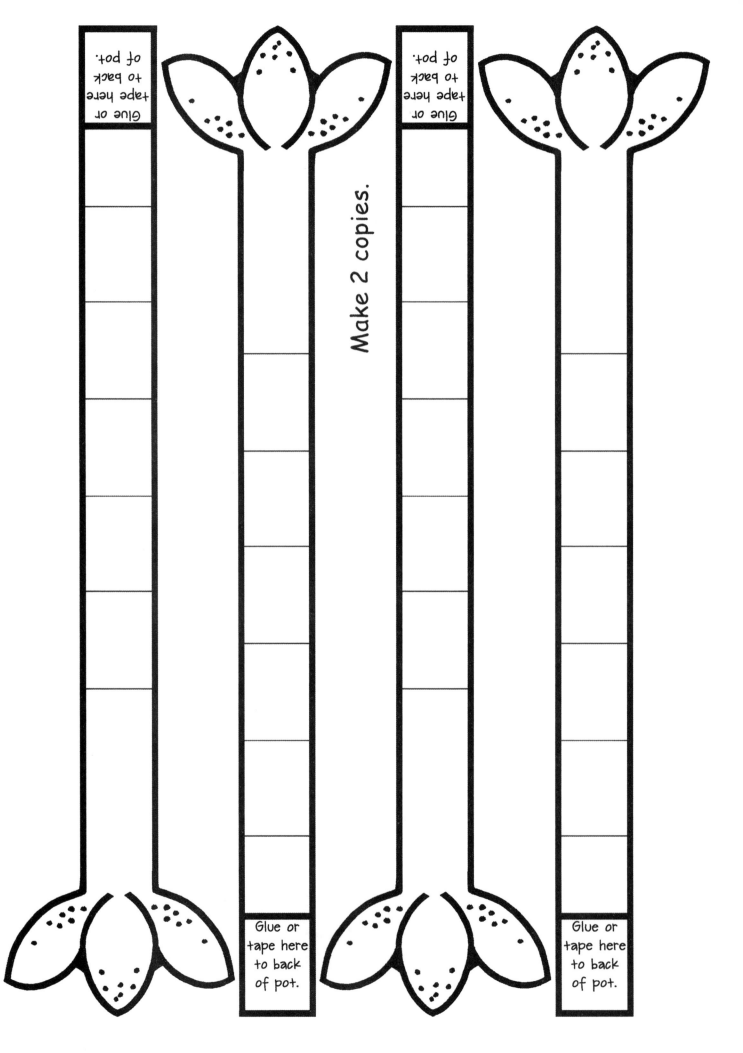

Make 2 copies.

Glue or
tape here
to back
of pot.

Glue or
tape here
to back
of pot.

When I pay my ten percent, I know my money is well spent.

I will not cheat the grocery clerk if he gives me too much change.

When I listen to lessons about Jesus, I am reverent.

Telling the truth helps others to trust me.

I can ask others not to use bad language around me.

I will love my family by helping with family home evening.

My lips are sealed when it comes to swearing or using bad words.

When I obey my parents, I always feel good.

I will watch good things on television and turn off the bad.

When I take the sacrament, I will think of Jesus.

I will read books that help me think of good things.

I will attend church and listen to the words that are said.

If my friends go to a bad movie, I will stay home.

I will get my work done on Saturday so I can keep the Sabbath day holy.

I will put good food into my body and throw away the rest.

I will treat my brothers and sisters kindly.

I will exercise and eat right to be healthy and feel good.

I will love others as Jesus taught and be a good Samaritan.

I choose not to use drugs or alcohol because my life is a gift.

I will play with those who have my same standards.

When I see someone in need, I will try to get them help.

Theme 11   My Faith in Jesus Christ Blesses My Life—
                 I Am Thankful for My Blessings

Scripture to Memorize:
Memorize *D&C 59:7* using visual on right.

Activity: Priesthood Power Branches & Blessings

OBJECTIVE—To Learn How the Priesthood Blesses Us: Children will learn about the priesthood, which comes from Jesus Christ. They will learn about the two branches of the priesthood, about the power and blessings that come from each, and about the duties of each priesthood office.

Bite-size Memorize

Thou ⊘+t
thank the 👤 Lord
th+👁 God
in all things.

D&C 59:7

TO MAKE VISUALS: Copy, color, and cut out the *Jesus Tree* and *Priesthood Branches*, leaf wordstrips, and fruit. Mount the tree and branches on a poster and laminate the entire poster. Place fruit and leaves to the left and right around the room.

ACTIVITY:
Focus on *More Lesson Ideas* #3 on the following page.

· Tell children that Joseph Smith prayed to Heavenly Father to know how to be baptized into His Church. Jesus Christ, through John the Baptist, gave Joseph Smith the priesthood to baptize others. Through His servants, Jesus gave Joseph Smith many other saving ordinances that can help us return to Heavenly Father.

· Beginning at age 12, men can receive the priesthood from an ordained priesthood holder (point to Jesus on the tree trunk and to the two priesthood divisions).

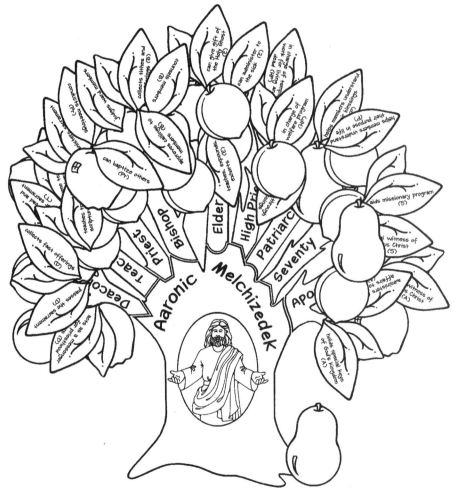

PHASE 1 (Puzzle Branches):

Talk about the two divisions in the priesthood, and their duties as follows:

• *The Aaronic Priesthood* can be held by boys beginning at age 12. The first office is DEACON. A deacon can pass the sacrament, gather fast offerings, and assist the bishop in caring for others. In the office of TEACHER, a boy does the same duties as a deacon but can also prepare the sacrament bread and water, and assist in home teaching. A young man in the office of PRIEST can do all the duties of a deacon and teacher, and can also bless the sacrament, baptize, and ordain others to the offices of deacon and teacher.

• *The Melchizedek Priesthood* offices are: ELDER, HIGH PRIEST, PATRIARCH, SEVENTY, and APOSTLE. The Melchizedek Priesthood is the higher priesthood. Melchizedek Priesthood holders can bless the sick, give special blessings to family members, give the gift of the Holy Ghost, and ordain others to the priesthood (shown on the leaves). Talk about how the priesthood brings us many blessings.

PHASE 2 (Build Tree):

Have children take turns doing the following.

1. Choose a leaf with a priesthood duty, read it, and place it on the appropriate side of the tree, e.g., Aaronic or Melchizedek. See *Answers* below.

2. Then choose a piece of fruit to place next to the leaf and tell how we are blessed from receiving this ordinance. Example: "passing the sacrament" (on the leaf) reminds us of the blessings that come from partaking of the sacrament (e.g., getting closer to Jesus, feeling His love, and remembering our baptismal covenants to help us choose the right).

Answers: To help children place the right duties with the right priesthood, follow the initials found on each leaf that follows: (D), (T), (Pr), (B), (E), (HP), (P), (S) and (A).

More Lesson Ideas (teach the theme using the concepts below and the above activity):

1. **I am thankful for my home and family** (Genesis 37, 41-45; "I Thank Thee, Dear Father," *Children's Songbook*, 7); "For Thy Bounteous Blessings," *Children's Songbook*, 21).

2. **I am thankful for my membership in the Church of Jesus Christ** (Mosiah 18:7-17; 3 Nephi 26:17-21; D&C 115:3-6; *Gospel Principles*, chapter 17).

3. **I am thankful for the priesthood, and I am blessed by it** ("Aaronic Priesthood," "Melchizedek Priesthood," and "Priesthood," *True to the Faith*, 3-4, 101-2, 124-28; *Gospel Principles*, chapter 13). You may want to explain that priesthood ordinances will help us return to our Heavenly Father, and read the following quote: "The Church bears his name. All ordinance work done in the Church is done in the name of Jesus Christ by those who bear the priesthood, i.e., who hold this power of Jesus Christ" (Elder Theodore M. Burton, Conference Report, October 1970).

4. **I will show my gratitude and love for Heavenly Father and Jesus Christ by keeping Their commandments** (Joshua 24:15; Proverbs 29:18; John 14:15; *Gospel Principles*, chapter 35).

Thou 🥐+t thank the Lord th+👁 God in all things.

D&C 59:7

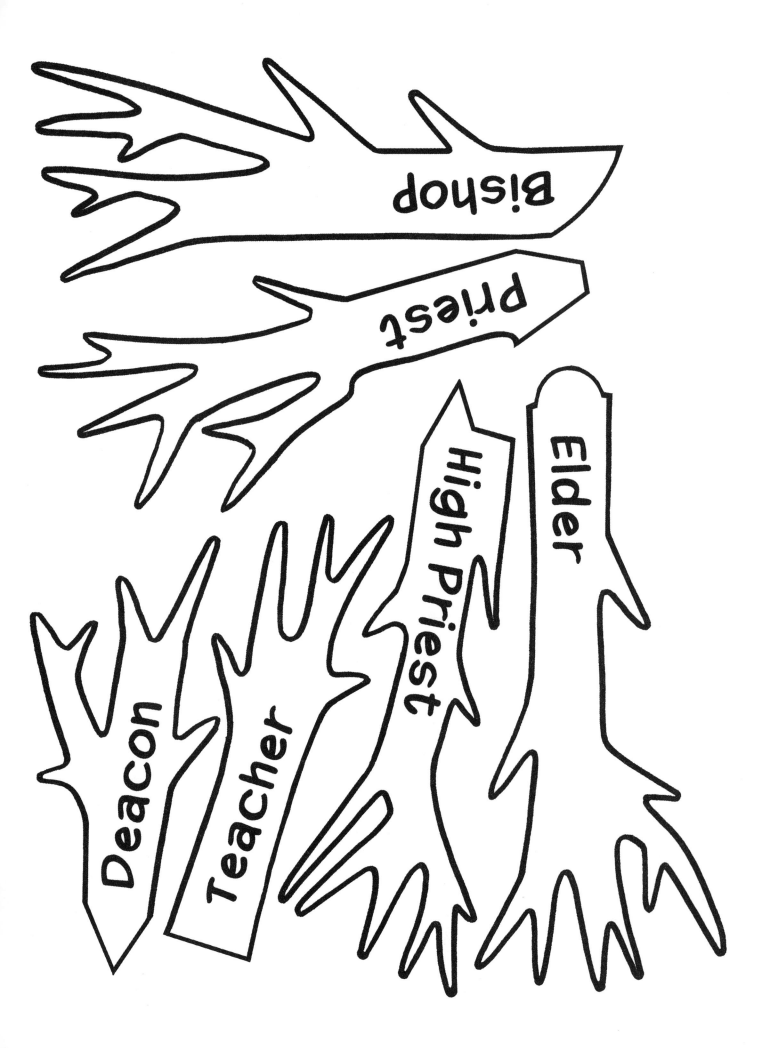

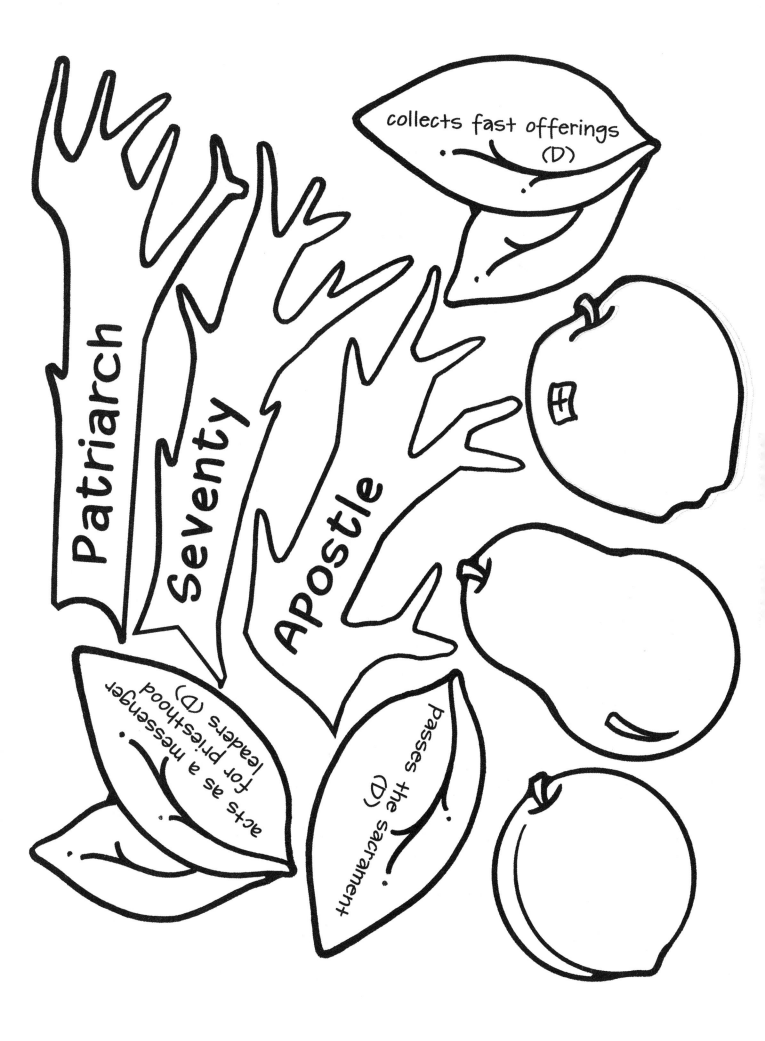

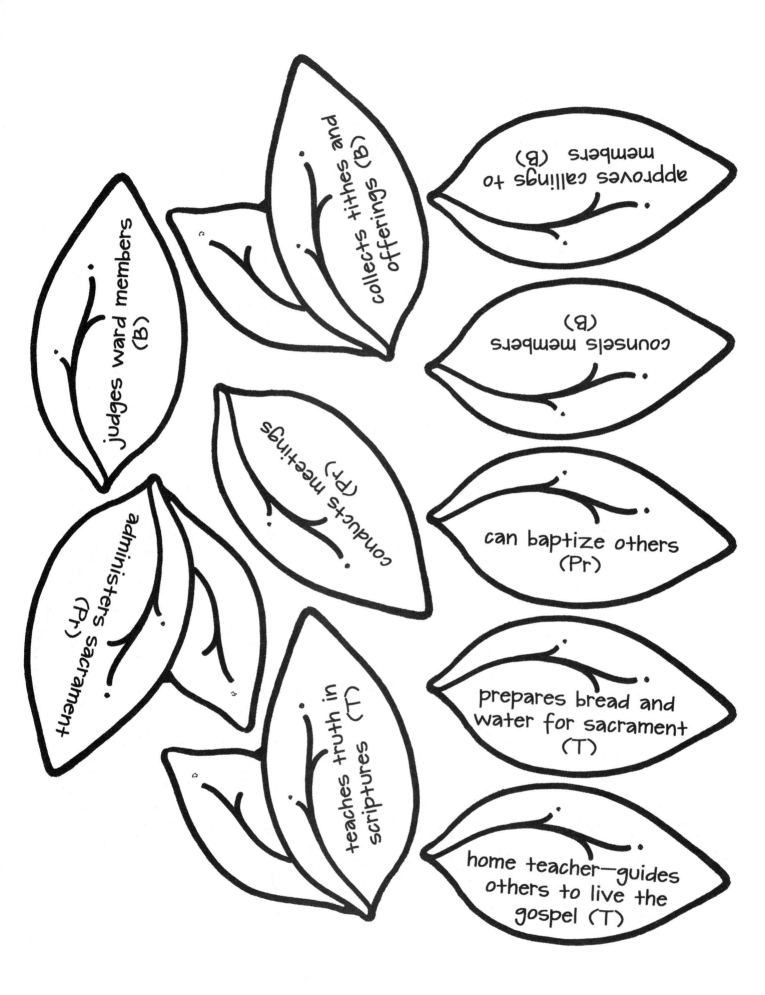

collects tithes and offerings (B)

approves callings to members (B)

judges ward members (B)

counsels members (B)

conducts meetings (Pr)

can baptize others (Pr)

administers sacrament (Pr)

prepares bread and water for sacrament (T)

teaches truth in scriptures (T)

home teacher—guides others to live the gospel (T)

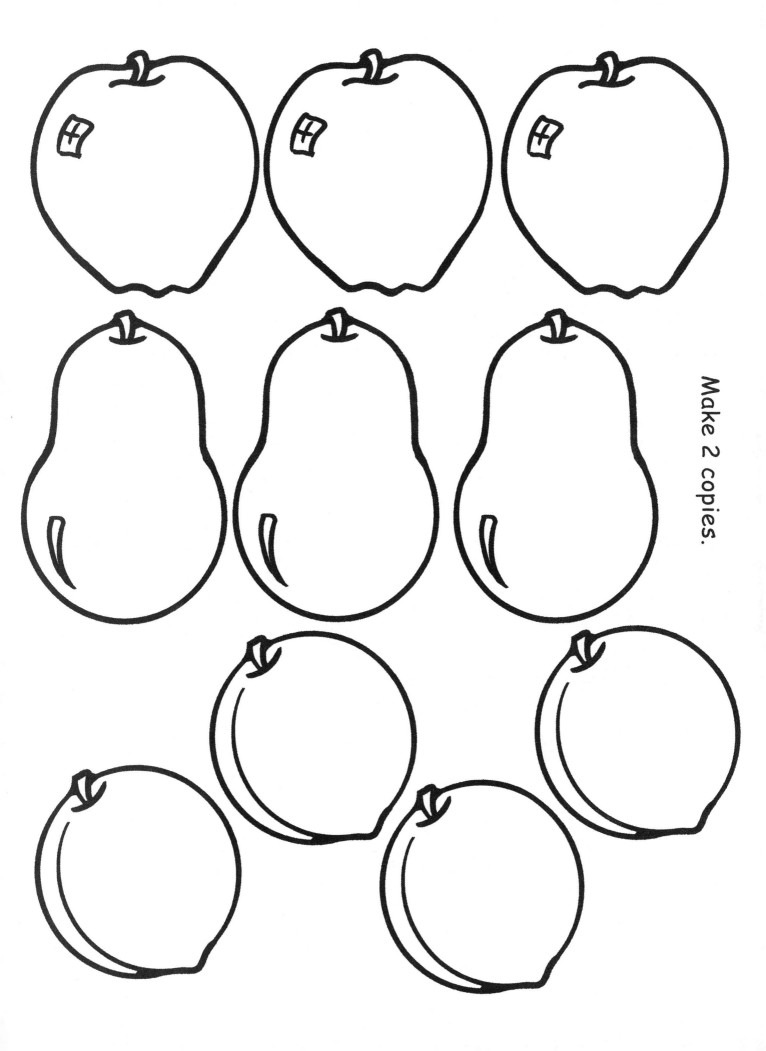

Make 2 copies.

Theme 12   Jesus Christ Once Lived on the Earth, and I Have Faith That He Will Come Again

Scripture to Memorize:

Memorize *Acts 1:11* using visual shown right.

Activity: Timeline to Second Coming

OBJECTIVE—To Learn How Prophets Testified of Jesus' Life:
Children will learn about the prophecies concerning Jesus Christ. Read *More Lesson Ideas* #1-4 on the following page. Read 2 Nephi 26:3 (signs to be given of Messiah's birth, death, resurrection).

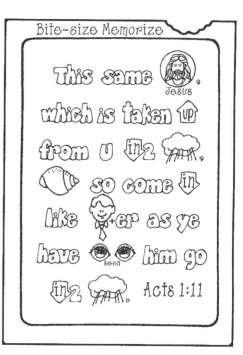

Bite-size Memorize

This same (Jesus), which is taken UP from U IN2 ☁, ☁ so come IN like er as ye have 👀 seen him go IN2 ☁. Acts 1:11

Prophecies About Jesus

His Birth   His Ministry   His Atonement and Death   His Resurrection   His Visit to the Nephites   His Second Coming

TO MAKE VISUALS:

1. Copy, color, and cut out the *Prophecies Tell About Jesus* pictures and prophecy cards. Place cards in a stack or container to draw from. Laminate two posters to display images vertically, using double-stick tape to mount images on posters (as shown).

ACTIVITY:

1. Read 2 Nephi 25:26 to children, saying that the prophets "talk of Christ," "rejoice in Christ," "preach of Christ," "prophesy of Christ," and write according to their prophecies so that we may know who will redeem us from our sins.

2. Introduce timeline by saying, "Let's go on a journey to visit the prophets that testified of Jesus Christ. Let's imagine what it would be like to be a child listening to the prophets when they tell about Jesus, who is to come."

3. With the images displayed at the top of the board, tell children that this is a timeline showing Jesus' life on earth. Read from the left to right and talk about each event. Ask children what they know about each picture.

4. Ask them to pretend they are in a time machine going back in time to listen to the prophets prophesy. Point to the *Prophecies Tell About Jesus* sign as you introduce the activity.

5. Have children read the prophecy cards and place them under the matching picture. Refer to the answers that follow. *Option:* As you reach the different places and time zones (e.g., New Testament, Book of Mormon, and Latter Days), you could mention that you are in that time zone.

ANSWERS (TO PROPHECY CARDS):

BIRTH: Helaman 14:2, Alma 7:9-10   **MINISTRY:** Isaiah 40:10-11, Mosiah 3:5

DEATH & ATONEMENT: 1 Nephi 11:33, Alma 5:48, Alma 7:13

RESURRECTION: Helaman 14:15, Hosea 13:14, Alma 7:12

VISIT TO NEPHITES: 2 Nephi 26:1, John 10:16, 3 Nephi 11:8-10

SECOND COMING: D&C 45:44, Joseph Smith—Matthew 1:28-36, D&C 45:16, 58-59

More Lesson Ideas (teach the theme using the concepts below and the above activity):

1. **Ancient prophets foretold the coming of the Savior to the earth** (Isaiah 7:14; 9:6-7; Helaman 14:2 "Jesus Christ, Prophecies about," in Topical Guide, 252-53; "Samuel Tells of the Baby Jesus," *Children's Songbook*, 36). You may also want to read 2 Nephi 26:3 (signs to be given of the Messiah's birth, death, and resurrection).

2. **The Savior Jesus Christ came to earth as a baby born in Bethlehem** (Luke 2:1-40; "Picture a Christmas" and "Away in a Manger," *Children's Songbook*," 50-51, 42-43).

3. **I can have peace, happiness, and love because of the coming of Jesus Christ** (Acts 1:9-11; "Second Coming of Jesus Christ," *True to the Faith*, 159-61; *Gospel Principles*, chapter 43).

4. **As I follow Jesus Christ in faith, I prepare myself for the Second Coming** (Matthew 25:1-13; D&C 45:56-59; 39:20-24)

This same Jesus, which is taken up from U in2 (cloud), so come in like +er as ye have seen him go in2 (cloud). Acts 1:11

His Birth

His Ministry

His Atonement and Death

His Resurrection

His Visit to the Nephites

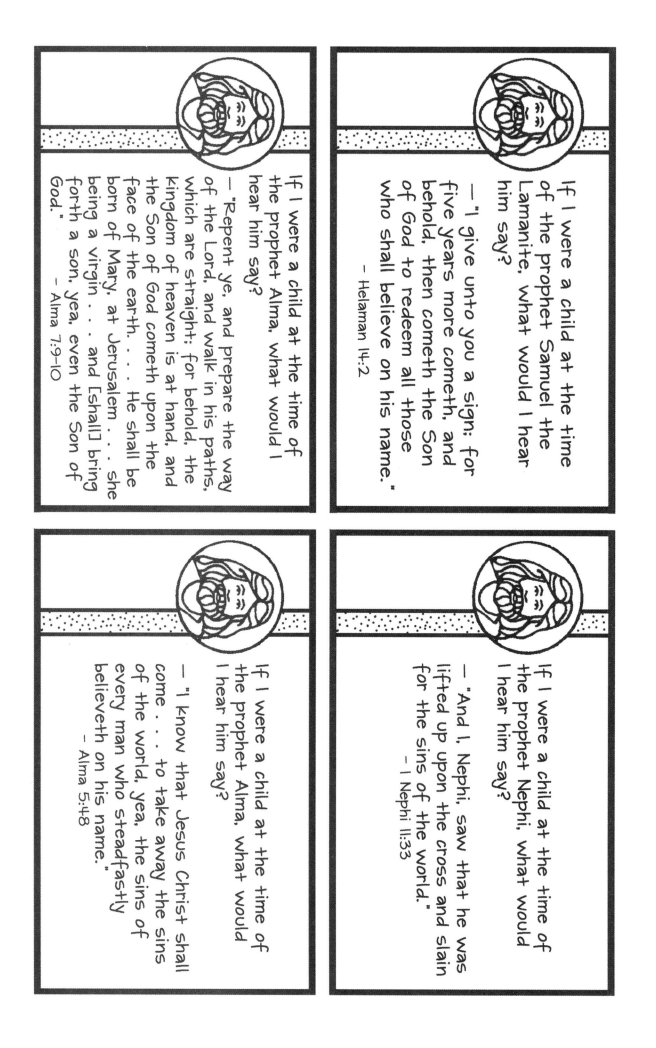

If I were a child at the time of the prophet Samuel the Lamanite, what would I hear him say?

— "I give unto you a sign: for five years more cometh, and behold, then cometh the Son of God to redeem all those who shall believe on his name."
— Helaman 14:2

If I were a child at the time of the prophet Nephi, what would I hear him say?

— "And I, Nephi, saw that he was lifted up upon the cross and slain for the sins of the world."
— 1 Nephi 11:33

If I were a child at the time of the prophet Alma, what would I hear him say?

— "Repent ye, and prepare the way of the Lord, and walk in his paths, which are straight; for behold, the kingdom of heaven is at hand, and the Son of God cometh upon the face of the earth . . . He shall be born of Mary, at Jerusalem . . . she being a virgin . . . and [shall] bring forth a son, yea, even the Son of God."
— Alma 7:9-10

If I were a child at the time of the prophet Alma, what would I hear him say?

— "I know that Jesus Christ shall come . . . to take away the sins of the world, yea, the sins of every man who steadfastly believeth on his name."
— Alma 5:48

If I were a child at the time of the prophet Isaiah, what would I hear him say?

— "Behold, the Lord GOD will come with strong [hand], and his arm shall rule for him: behold, his reward is with him, and his work before him. He shall feed his flock like a shepherd: he shall gather the lambs with his arm, and carry them in his bosom, and shall gently lead those that are with young."

— Isaiah 40:10-11

If I were a child at the time of the prophet King Benjamin, what would I hear him say?

— "For behold, the time cometh . . . that . . . the Lord . . . shall come down . . . among the children of men, . . . and shall go forth amongst men, working mighty miracles, such as healing the sick, raising the dead, causing the lame to walk, the blind to receive their sight, and the deaf to hear, and curing all manner of diseases."

— Mosiah 3:5

If I were a child at the time of the prophet Alma, what would I hear him say?

— "The Son of God suffereth according to the flesh that he might take upon him the sins of his people, that he might blot out their transgressions according to the power of his deliverance; and now behold, this is the testimony which is in me."

— Alma 7:13

If I were a child at the time of the prophet Samuel the Lamanite, what would I hear him say?

— Jesus "must die that salvation may come . . . to bring to pass the resurrection of the dead, that thereby men may be brought into the presence of the Lord."

— Helaman 14:15

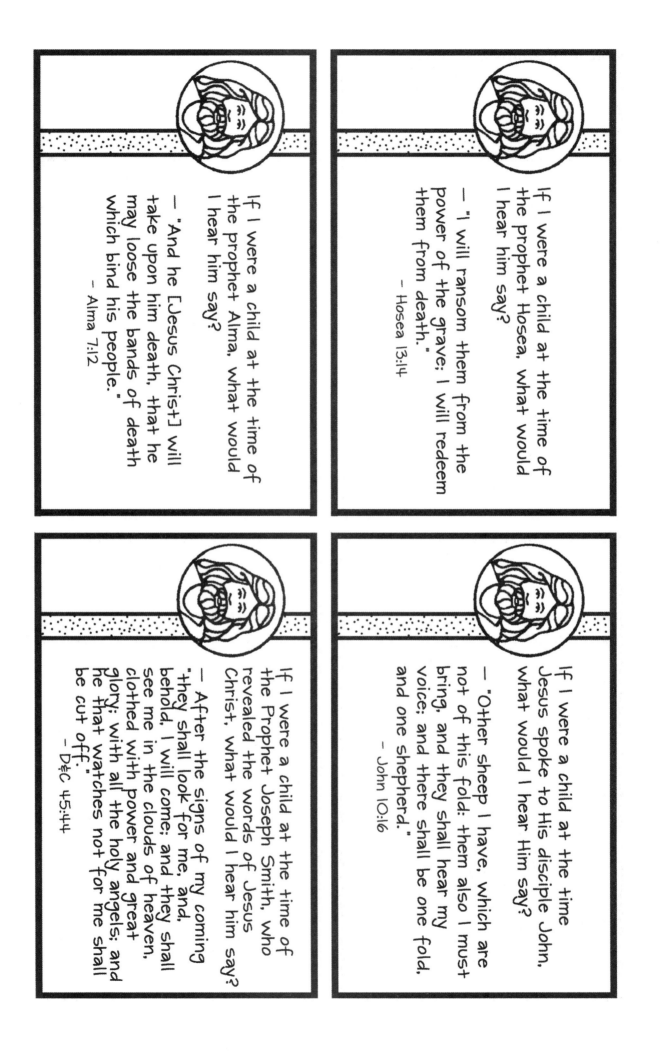

If I were a child at the time of the prophet Hosea, what would I hear him say?

— "I will ransom them from the power of the grave; I will redeem them from death."

— Hosea 13:14

If I were a child at the time of the prophet Alma, what would I hear him say?

— "And he [Jesus Christ] will take upon him death, that he may loose the bands of death which bind his people."

— Alma 7:12

If I were a child at the time Jesus spoke to His disciple John, what would I hear Him say?

— "Other sheep I have, which are not of this fold: them also I must bring, and they shall hear my voice; and there shall be one fold, and one shepherd."

— John 10:16

If I were a child at the time of the Prophet Joseph Smith, who revealed the words of Jesus Christ, what would I hear him say?

— "After the signs of my coming "they shall look for me, and, behold, I will come; and they shall see me in the clouds of heaven, clothed with power and great glory; with all the holy angels; and he that watches not for me shall be cut off."

— D&C 45:44

If I were a child at the time of the prophet Nephi, son of Helaman, what would I hear him say?

— "They cast their eyes up again towards heaven; and behold, they saw a Man descending out of heaven; and he was clothed in a white robe; and he came down and stood in the midst of them; and the eyes of the whole multitude were turned upon him . . . And . . . he stretched forth his hand and spake unto the people, saying: Behold, I am Jesus Christ, whom the prophets testified shall come into the world." — 3 Nephi 11:8–10

If I were a child at the time of the prophet Nephi, what would I hear him say?

— "And after Christ shall have risen from the dead he shall show himself unto you, my children, and my beloved brethren; and the words which he shall speak unto you shall be the law which ye shall do."
— 2 Nephi 26:1

If I were a child at the time of the Prophet Joseph Smith, telling of the coming of Jesus, what would I hear him say?

— After "wars . . . famines . . . pestilences . . . earthquakes . . . the love of men shall wax cold; . . . this Gospel . . . shall be preached in all the world, . . . the sun shall be darkened, and the moon shall not give her light, and the stars shall fall from heaven, and the powers of heaven shall be shaken. . . . Then shall appear the sign of the Son of Man in heaven . . . coming in the clouds of heaven, . . . with power and great glory."
— Joseph Smith—Matthew 1:28–36

If I were a child at the time of the Prophet Joseph Smith, who revealed the words of Jesus Christ, what would I hear him say?

— "In the day when I shall come in my glory in the clouds of heaven, to fulfil the promises that I have made unto your fathers. . . . The earth shall be given unto them for an inheritance; and they shall multiply and wax strong, and their children shall grow up without sin unto salvation. For the Lord shall be in their midst, and his glory shall be upon them, and he will be their king and their lawgiver."
— D&C 45:16, 58–59

THE FOLLOWING PRODUCTS ALSO CORRELATE WITH THE 2007 PRIMARY THEME:
I'll Follow Him in Faith

These books are also on CD-ROM so you can print images in color or black-and-white. *Singing Fun* and the *Sing-Along* video (not shown) will help you teach theme songs for the 2007 year.

Primary Partners Singing Fun

You will find visuals to teach songs for the following themes:

1. I'll Follow Him in Faith
2. This Is My Beloved Son
3. I'm Trying to Be like Jesus
4. I Know That My Redeemer Lives
5. An Angel Came to Joseph Smith
6. I Want to Live the Gospel
7. Love Is Spoken Here
8. Listen, Listen

Primary Partners Sharing Time Treasures

You will find 55 activities for themes 1-12:

- Faithful Saints (Guessing Game)
- Plan of Salvation (Storyboard)
- Miracles of Jesus (Poster)
- Faithful Footsteps (Flip-Chart)
- Sabbath Day (Calendar)
- Atonement (Object Lesson)
- Always Remember Jesus (Covenant Reminder)
- Sacrament Symbols (Puzzle)
- Follow Jesus (List)
- Gifts to Jesus (Service Advent)
- Priesthood Power Lines (Puzzle)

. . . And more!

More Sharing Time or FHE Ideas
to Match Most "I'll Follow Him in Faith" Themes

The following books are in full color. Simply tear out, cut out, and enjoy games and activities to motivate gospel learning. Also available for each is a CD-ROM to print the images.

Jesus Loves Me—Gospel Activities:

- Following Jesus' Light   • Jesus Blesses Me with His Teachings   • Jesus Restored His Church
- Jesus Saved Me from Physical and Spiritual Death
- Jesus Showed His Love   • Heavenly Father Promised to Send Jesus   • Honoring Jesus
- My Faith Increases As I Learn about Jesus
- The Sacrament Helps Me Remember Jesus' Love

Gospel Fun Activities:

- Blessings of the Temple   • Consequences
- Family History   • Follow the Examples of Jesus
- Happy Family   • Invite the Spirit
- Jesus Will Come Again   • My Body Is a Temple
- Preparing for the Temple and a Mission   • Prophets
- Sabbath Day   • Stand as a Witness

More Sharing Time of FHE Ideas
to Match Most "I'll Follow Him in Faith" Themes

The following books are in full color. Simply tear out, cut out, and enjoy games and activities to motivate gospel learning. Also available for each is a CD-ROM to print the images.

Tons of Fun! Gospel Activities:

- Bless My Family • Child of God
- Choose the Right • Following Jesus
- Following the Prophet
- Gifts to Jesus • Gospel Standards
- Listen and Obey • Repentance
- Responsible Family • Temple Blessings

Fun in a Flash! Gospel Activities:

- Accountability • Choose the Right
- Commandments • Faith • Follow Jesus
- The Holy Ghost • Missionary Talents
- Missionary Work • Repentance
- Second Coming • Service • Testimony

Enjoy More Full-Color, Ready-to-Use Books and CD-ROMS:

With these colored, ready-to-use visuals, you can create memorable learning activities and motivate children to sing and learn in family home evening and Primary. They are also available on CD-ROM so you can print images in color or black-and-white.

Super Singing Activities

You'll find Animal and Insect Do as I'm Doing, Bird in the Leafy Treetops, Build a Prophet, Build a Snowman, Christmas Tree Sing with Me, City of Enoch Meter, Fill Noah's Ark, Follow the Signs, Going Fishing! Keyword Connection, Melody's Family Tree, Name that Tune, Singing Simon, Sunny Sunday Sounds, Temple Flowers "Bee" a Singer, and more.

Super Little Singers

You'll find singing motivators, visuals, and action activities for 28 songs (21 from the *Children's Songbook*). Enjoy using the visuals for these seven all-time favorite children's songs: Ants Go Marching, Eensy Weensy Spider, Five Little Ducks, Five Little Speckled Frogs, Old MacDonald, Twinkle, Twinkle, Little Star, and Wheels on the Bus.